GET UP,
GET OUT,
& GET A LIFE!

It Ain't Over Til I Say It's Over...

Pink Lady

Pink Lady Productions
Woodland Hills, CA

Published in the USA by
Pink Lady Productions
P.O. Box 5184
Woodland Hills, CA 91307

Softcover Edition
ISBN: 978-0-692-75607-2

Table of Contents

Prologue:
IT'S EASY BEING PINK   7

Section One:
GET UP (Where There's a Life, There's a Story)   15
    The Birth of an Attitude
    The Early Years
    The Second Time Around
    The "Pink Lady" Is Born
    A New Twist in a Perfect World
    Onward and Upward
    Courage for a New Life
    Cruising with an Attitude
    Aging with an Attitude
    Getting an Attitude Adjustment

Section Two:
GET OUT (Learn to Live Longer, Better, and Wiser)   71
    Moving On
    Life Is for the Living
    Get Ready, Get Set, Get Out
    Think Positive – Go For It!
    Building Blocks for Getting Out
    Negative to Positive Communication
    Volunteer – Help Yourself by Helping Others
    Thoughts to Live By
    Exercises to Help Achieve Your Goals
    One Step at a Time
    Resolutions – Making It All Happen
    Secrets for Staying Young
    Tips to Increase Your Willpower
    Mind Over Matter

Section Three:
GET IT ON (Senior Sexuality and Relationships)   **111**

> *Can We Talk?*
> *What's "It" All About?*
> *Love Is in the Air*
> *"You've Come a Long Way, Baby!"*
> *Wise Words for Senior Dating*
> *Finding the Humor in Dating*
> *Places to Meet that Special Someone*
> *Let's Talk About Romance*
> *Keeping the Joy of Romance Going*
> *Reaching the Point of No Return*
> *The Heat Continues – In Bed*
> *Ideas for Romancing the Aging Lover*
> *All that Glitters Is Not Gold*

Section Four:
GET A LIFE (Fabulous at Any Age)   **167**

> *Now Is the Best Time*
> *Ways to Reach for and Grab Hold of the Stars*
> *The Art of Re-Invention*
> *Re-Invention Is Not Just a Word*
> *The Other "R" Words*
> *The Senior Pageant*
> *Get A Life! Seminars*
> *Hollywood Calls – "A Star Is Born"*
> *Rockin' with the Ages*

Epilogue:
IT AIN'T OVER TIL I SAY IT'S OVER   **231**

DEDICATION

I am very proud to dedicate my life's story to the "young at heart" who realize that no matter what age they are, they continue their journeys through life being vital, creative, and productive.

Living life to the "max" with energy, enthusiasm, and excitement is definitely worth our commitment, dedication, and passion; every moment, every hour, every day. By experiencing this, you have the best reason to

"GET UP, GET OUT, & GET A LIFE!"

Prologue:
IT'S EASY BEING PINK

Kermit the Frog said, "It's not easy being green." But I say loud and clear, "It *is* easy being pink!" To feel the energy and aura of beauty that a color can give helps people see life through rose-colored glasses.

What a wonderful world we live in! I am awed by the fact that at 84 years *young*, I'm able to enjoy my journey now more than ever. I have an incredibly active and productive life. And I owe it all to my positive attitude.

Having such an attitude can work wonders! It can make or break a whole lifetime of living – just ask me. Ever since I can remember, I've had an upbeat, positive outlook which has unequivocally led me to live in such a way as to not let anyone or anything rain on my parade.

What would you call the stage of life between the ages of 60 and 100? Some would call it the declining years. That's nonsense! I call it wonderful!

I'm Jackie Goldberg, known to everyone as *The Pink Lady*, and I believe that now is the time to *Get Up, Get Out, & Get a Life!* If you truly want to live life to its fullest, I challenge you to read on. Trust me, it just might be the best decision you could ever make!

This truly is the very best time of my life. Being a "young senior" is like living in a new world. I'm so excited about this book – it's my first – and I'm hoping it will show all my fellow baby boomers and senior friends that life doesn't stop when you turn 60. I also want to prove to the younger generations that contrary to what you may have heard, you don't stop living at that age. Believe me, there is a lot of living to look forward to.

We've all heard the song *What's Love Got to Do With It?* I have my own version called *What's Age Got to Do With It?* I believe you are only as old as you want to be. Right now I'm enjoying the freedom to reinvent myself. I have a whole new outlook on what life can be – adventurous and downright fabulous! We can do whatever we want, go wherever we please, and be whomever we choose to be. Anything and everything is possible.

I've always been the kind of person to *Get Up, Get Out, & Get a Life*, now more than ever. My life has been a continuous and exciting roller-coaster ride, and it's still rolling along at breakneck speed. You might say that I am a "survivor" of life. To me, life is precious – every moment, of every hour, of every day. I intend to make the most of it, and so should you!!

I believe I'm a perfect example of what the right attitude can do for you. You need to know who you are and realize that there is still a lot of livin' to do. The purpose of life, after all, is to live it. This is truly our time to live life to the max – to taste each experience and to live in the present moment – wisely, lovingly and with enthusiasm.

The first thing I do when I wake up every morning is sit up, put my legs over the edge of the bed, look out the window into my lovely garden and say "thank you" to the Universe for giving me another day. It's a fabulous feeling to know that I have a chance to begin a joyous and fulfilling new chapter in my life by helping others see life through rose-colored glasses.

I seem to recall the illustrious Bette Davis saying, "Getting older is not for sissies." And I say, "In today's world, it takes guts to get older, without being old." Aging happens to everyone. It's inevitable. However there's no need to become a victim of age. We should be thinking of ways to celebrate getting older by using the wisdom we have gathered through our past experiences.

I can remember my grandparents at 59 and 65. In those days they were considered "over the hill" and ready for the dreaded rocking chair. Today, that age group is called "late middle age," and many of them are still working, going back to college and starting second and even third careers. It's normal today for people in their 60s, 70s and 80s to continue their education and quest for knowledge in areas outside their previously chosen fields. A phenomenal change in the way people live and retire has occurred just in the past 50 years.

As seniors living in the 21st century, our demeanor, our appearance, and most important, our attitudes are helping us live longer and feel more confident about ourselves. We look younger, are more active and better educated. We are definitely more independent and more in tune with world events than ever before.

Today we use the internet for everything... email, social media, games, banking, work-related projects, and of course, dating services! Cupid and I can both tell you this is no time to call it quits when it comes to romance. This is a time to embrace life and all the exciting opportunities it can offer. My zest for living, my positive perspective and my unending energy and enthusiasm are giving me the life I've always wanted. Thank you, God!

There are a number of people in the entertainment industry over the age of 70 who are still performing, creating, and utilizing their own positive energies. I believe it was Clint Eastwood (86), well known actor, director and producer who once said, "In

Hollywood, if you're over 50, you're history." Well, he himself has proven just how wrong that statement was.

Dame Judi Dench (81), Cloris Leachman (90), Angela Lansbury (90), Maggie Smith (81), Tony Bennett (90) and of course, Betty White (94) – are all examples of the robust over 60 crowd living their lives to the fullest.

As we get older, we tend to make life simpler, for we realize we don't need to play as many notes in order to sing the same song. Age gives us the "perfect pitch" to simplify our role in life. We must have the courage, the conviction, the dedication and the passion to believe in who we are and what we want to accomplish in these, the best years of our lives!

One must have a strong sense of self-esteem at any age. However by the time we hit 60, we do not have to prove to anyone how resilient we are, because we just are. I mean, we've made it this far! We have arrived at a time of life where we are free to spread our wings and soar as high as we want.

For me, a 24-hour day is simply not enough time to accomplish everything I want to do. So I've had to learn an important lesson – time must be controlled and directed in order to make you a happier and more productive person. You can start by not watching others live their lives, but by concentrating on how you live yours. You should make your daily goals realistic ones. If you do one new thing each day or each week, and don't overload yourself, you will succeed in accomplishing what you set out to do. That old saying, "If at first you don't succeed, try, try again" is so true!

Someone once said, "Life may not be the party we'd hoped for, but while we're here, we might as well dance." Edward Elliot has said, "By being yourself, you put something wonderful in the world that was never there before." I myself say, "Live, love and laugh your way through these, the best years of your life."

We all need to love the age we are. We're only here once – enjoy it, embrace it and live it. It's never too late! Think of your birthdays as just numbers – starting places to begin new chapters for enjoying your life even more than before.

I am now, at age 84, my own best friend. My strength, understanding and compassion for those around me have made me a better person, and I have the freedom to do all the things I only dreamed of doing in the past. If you're thinking of reinventing yourself so that life doesn't pass you by, rest assured – it can be done.

In the chapters to follow, I will share my personal stories and ideas on how I believe everyone can live their best life right now, today, and be who they are – not what others want them to be or think they should be. Believe me, it's not always easy, but it can be done just by taking one step at a time. I will show you what I have achieved by utilizing a positive attitude, so that you too can realize your own goals and dreams.

Remember, life's a journey. Grab hold of it! Open your mind and your heart to it! Live it and love it... before you leave it!

You are beginning a personal journey.
At times you may expect the answers to come quickly,
but try to be patient;
some answers may take a lifetime
to be revealed to you.

Though you may be a little uncertain now
and your confidence may be shaken,
you will stand on your own feet soon enough.
Your legs will grow to be strong under you;
they will take you where you want to go.

You'll make mistakes along the way;
a fork in the road may present a path
that you later decide was the wrong way to go.
Take the time to learn from your mistakes,
but don't be too hard on yourself.

You are learning to make your own choices,
and there is great joy in that.
You are a human being who is embarking
on the important journey of discovering
who you are and what you have to offer.

Celebrate your uniqueness,
and you will triumph on your life's journey.

~ Deborah Weinberg

Section One:
GET UP – Where There's a Life, There's a Story

Jacqueline Helen Rigmont, age 2

The Birth of an Attitude

It all started nearly 80 years ago in a small town outside of Boston, Massachusetts called Melrose. "Jackie, come down from that tree before you get hurt," my mother would yell at the top of her voice. Dressed in a wrap-around floral dress circa 1936, it was her daily exercise to get her tomboyish four-year-old towheaded little girl to behave. I eventually came down... after all, one has to eat, even at four.

I was definitely a star in the making, even then, as I began playing dress-up in my mother's clothes. I believe who we are really begins at an early stage in our lives. That's when our characters and personalities are formed. This becomes the foundation of our persona. My mom and dad were childhood sweethearts who married at the age of 16 in December 1931. Their

Mom and Dad's wedding, 1931

16

marriage lasted 62 wondrous years. Wow! We can't say that about too many marriages today.

These were the times of The Depression. We were poor in the sense that we didn't have a lot of money, but we were definitely rich due to having a close-knit, warm and loving family. We lived with my grandparents at the time, and that provided me with a built-in audience for my acting career. To them, I was always a star.

With my parents, Fran and Scotty Rigmont, and sister Marilyn, 1942

My first audience was made up of those who helped my grandfather make a living. You see, he was a "junk man." He had a horse and wagon and would go out every morning and drive up and down the streets of our town yelling, "Rags? Any rags for sale?" When I would venture out with him, which was always fun and exciting, I too would yell out loud and clear, "Rags! Please! Rags – or anything else for sale?" Thus began my training for the stage.

At three years old, my parents gave me what they called in those days elocution lessons. Soon thereafter, I started to act. My first stage performance was at a Christmas pageant where I recited *The Night Before Christmas*. I was fantastic... well, at least that's what my mom and dad told me!

Acting in one of many high school plays, age 15

Throughout high school, I had all the leads in the school plays. And on our debate team, I won "Best Speaker" at every contest. Fact is, you couldn't keep me quiet then, and you can't keep me quiet now! I honestly attribute my self-confidence to my parents who always encouraged me to understand and appreciate who I was and go after whatever I wanted to accomplish. That confidence, along with my positive attitude, has kept me on the right path through good times and bad, and has guided me on many wonderful adventures along life's incredible journey. I believe I owe everything I've accomplished to that positive attitude and to my kind and caring parents.

Attitudes, like flowers, grow from seeds. They have to begin somewhere. I remember when my attitude was born. The year was 1936. It was a cold, rainy day. I was four years old. I can see myself as if it was yesterday. I was dressed in blue overalls, a long-sleeved pink sweater, a pink parka, and blue and pink rain boots. I was standing in the pouring rain at a bus stop in Melrose with my mother, who was eight months pregnant with my sister. We were on our way to see my dad at Boston County Hospital, where he was recovering from pneumonia – a one-hour trip from where we lived.

The bus stopped to pick us up and the driver leaned out. Noticing my mother's condition, he warned that we would have to stand for an hour or more, as the bus was completely full. My mother, who was holding my hand, started to walk away. Now, I can't remember what I had for breakfast this morning, but I do remember what happened next. I let go of my mother's hand and jumped onto the stairwell of the bus. With hands on hips I shouted to all the passengers in my best little rag-girl voice, "Isn't there a gentleman on this bus who will let a lady sit down?" With that, three men got up. The bus driver laughed. My mother and I boarded the bus and were able to sit comfortably the entire trip.

Jackie, age 4, and full of the right attitude!

My attitude came to life at that very moment. I believe that our attitudes can make the roads we travel either fun and exciting or boring and dull. They can make or break a whole lifetime of living. It's up to us which attitudes we let determine the way we live our lives.

High school graduation, age 17

The longer I live, the more I realize the impact of attitude on life. Having a positive attitude is one of the most important facets you can possess – more important than just about anything else. It influences everything we do and the manner in which we relate to our families, friends, school mates and co-workers. It most definitely has an impact on the very core of our social lives.

21

The remarkable thing is, we have a choice regarding the attitude we embrace for ourselves. We cannot change our past, nor can we change the inevitable. But we can change our attitude to enable us to live our lives in a positive and energetic way.

The Early Years

In those days it was expected that a young lady marry early. And I did. At age nineteen I married Irving Penn, a handsome Naval officer who was eight years

My wedding to Irving, 1951

older than I. Over the next seven years I gave birth to three children – two boys and a girl. Life wasn't always easy, but we managed to bring up our children in a warm and happy home, despite an accident which left Irving on disability. My parents, who were still young themselves, helped us out in so many ways – mostly financial.

My 3 children with Irving – Michael, Richard and Deborah

I took to being a homemaker and a mother. I was learning new things every day, just as my children were. My zest for life was just beginning. I remember being elected President of the Parent-Teachers Association for my son Michael's elementary school where I initiated the school's program of stage productions to make money for the PTA. Who knew this would be the beginning of a producing career that would blossom and flourish decades later when I reached my seventies?

I was always outgoing, and had a positive outlook. And I believe things happen for a reason. That attitude would soon be put to the ultimate test. With only a high-school diploma and three children under 10, life suddenly took a turn for the worse. After nine years of marriage, I suddenly became a widow. Irving unexpectedly died from a brain aneurism and I found myself at a crossroads.

Mom and Dad, always there for me

Thank God for my mom and dad who at that time were only in their late forties. My dad took my kids to music lessons, baseball practice and all the school events, while my mom took on the job of making sure they were fed, clean, did their homework and in bed on time. I was so lucky to have parents who had my best interest and welfare as a priority in their lives. Their help with my children allowed me to find work and go back to school. I knew in my mind and in my heart that my life, at that moment, had nowhere to go but up.

My first job – or should I say the first job I went after – was at the International House of Pancakes. I became "the hostess with the mostess." Now remember, I had never been employed; having gone straight from my parents' home to be with my husband at age 19. But I soon realized I had plenty of experience as a hostess. After all, did I not get my kids up every morning and greet them with a smile? Serve them breakfast, lunch and dinner, and clean up after them? I was a natural!

At the job interview, the first question that Margo asked me was, "Do you know how to work the copper register at the front of the restaurant?" Margo happened to be the head hostess for all of the IHOP restaurants.

Now, you really have to understand something: I have what I call chutzpah, which translates to "big-time attitude." So my answer to Margo's question, which happened to be my stock answer for every question asked of me, was, "Yes, of course I do!" In reality I had actually never worked a register before, but if that's what I had to do to get the job, I would do it!

Guess what? It worked! I got hired for my first job ever! My hours would be from 4pm to midnight, which was perfect. I could be with the children for most of the day, get them off to school, and see them when they got home. My parents, God bless them, would take over from the time I left for work until the kids went to bed.

The first night I went to work, everything was going along smoothly. I smiled at the customers as they walked in. I chatted with them as I escorted them to their table. I handed them the oversized menu – well, everything is oversized to me! I brought them water and continued to make small talk.

A few hours into my shift, Margo asked me to handle the register so she could take a dinner break. "Oh, no," I thought. "Not the register!" The register was the old copper type. It was huge – about two and a half feet wide with copper keys all over it. I stood there, praying that no one would come up to pay. But, as you know, that's not the way it works.

After a few minutes, one of the first couples I had seated came to the register with their bill in hand. I took it... I smiled... I smiled again... and asked them how their meal was. I continued to chat with them until the very nice gentleman countered, "As much as we like talking to you, Jackie, we need to pay our bill and leave."

Margo, out of the corner of her eye, must have observed the exchange. She came over and told me to return to the floor and she would take over. Moments later, she told me that she needed to speak with me before I left for the night. I knew I was in trouble.

When the time came, I approached Margo with my heart in my throat, certain that I was about to lose my first job. She sat me down and asked, "Jackie, you know nothing about the register, do you?" Tears welled up in my eyes, and I confessed softly, "No I don't." With that, Margo got up from her chair, came around the table, took me in her arms and reassured, "It's okay, honey. With your personality, your zest for life and your energy, I can teach you how to work the register, but I would never be able to teach you the positive attitude you have that has brought a smile to everyone here tonight. That is a gift that can't be taught. Welcome to IHOP!"

I really loved working at IHOP. But as enjoyable as it was, after about six months I realized I needed to find a better-paying job. So I left there and went to work as the head hostess at Delmonico's, a prestigious restaurant in Beverly Hills. My new hours were 12 to 3pm and 5 to 11pm. The job was great and the money was almost triple what I'd been making at IHOP. But the hours left me no time for a life.

I made most of my money in tips. I knew almost every customer by name, and they knew all about my three kids and how I was raising them alone. It seemed they all wanted to do whatever they could to help out. They also knew that I knew about their mistresses at lunch and their wives at dinner. They admired the fact that I was able to keep my family together under difficult circumstances while simultaneously maintaining a positive attitude and cheery personality.

Time was flying by and I was spending hardly any of it with my children. My parents and I agreed that I needed to go to school and learn a trade that would allow me to live a more normal life. That's when I thought of becoming a manicurist. That would provide me with a regular work schedule and allow for more time with my family. So began my new adventure.

I continued to work at Delmonico's, but my schedule was now modified. I would go to manicurist school from 7 to 11am; work at Delmonico's from 12 to 3pm; stay there while I studied my manicure manual from 3 to 5pm; continue working until midnight; then go home and study some more until 2 in the morning. I would then go to bed and get up at 6am to start all over again.

Remember, I was only in my late twenties, in good health and with a fantastic, attitude that assured me I could do it all. And I did! Even though it was a brutal schedule, I knew there was a rainbow at the end. And with the help of my mother and father, who really sacrificed their lives during this time by becoming surrogate parents to my kids, I knew we would survive.

No matter what our attitude is, there has to be a plan and an ability to adapt in order to make any life changes. That willingness to change our way of thinking about who we are, what we are doing, and where we are going, is vitally important. Here I was literally starting all over again.

So after eight and a half months of study and full-time work, I graduated from manicurist school. "Congratulations, Jackie! You're now a manicurist!" My family and all my friends were overjoyed to see me looking toward a brighter future. There I was, bright-eyed and bushy tailed, wearing a white uniform with a manicure kit in hand, and thrilled beyond words to have a new career.

I graduated from manicure school on a Thursday afternoon. I'll never forget what happened next. That same night, I read in the paper of an opening for a manicurist at Mary Ann Bowser's salon in the Beverly-Wilshire complex, one of the first and largest condominium complexes in the city. Well, was I not the "manicurist with the mostist?" The following day, I went to apply for the job. Beverly Hills, look out, here I come!

I arrived at 9am, manicure kit in hand, and sooo very excited. The owner, Mary Ann, told me I was early, that she was busy, and that I would have to wait until she was free, because the job interview included giving her a manicure. "No problem," I remember thinking.

As I sat in the salon, I noticed that the shop had two other manicurists and five hair stylists. The clientele, I observed, included a number of movie stars whom I recognized. I was getting more excited by the minute... and a bit nervous.

At 11:30, Mary Ann was ready for her manicure. Now, as you know, a regular manicure usually takes about 25 minutes, including a hand and arm massage. Well, one hour and 45 minutes later, I was finally finished. With a big smile, I looked up at Mary Ann and waited for a response. There was nothing but silence. She looked at me, looked down at her hands, then back up at me and announced, "This is the worst manicure I have ever had. How long have you been a manicurist?"

With tears rolling down my face, I glanced at my watch and responded, "18 hours and 42 minutes." With that, Mary Ann laughed. "My dear child," she added, "I can teach you how to be a good manicurist. All it takes is practice. But I could never teach you that wonderful spirit, joy for life, and dynamic personality that you naturally possess. It would be my pleasure to bring you on board and teach you."

Yes!!!

During my time at the salon, which catered mostly to the Hollywood elite, I learned the Juliet Margolin method of doing manicures from the renowned Grace of Beverly Hills. It was a specialized process that involved wrapping the nails in paper-thin gauze so they would grow and not break. Knowing this method allowed me to make double the money and secure a more prestigious clientele. By now I was adjusting to being a single mother with a full-time job. And with the remaining time I was able to raise my children – with the continuing wonderful help of my parents.

After working at Mary Ann's for a year and a half, including Saturdays, I secured a position with better hours and fewer days as a head manicurist at Cassey's on Rodeo Drive in Beverly Hills. I could now set my own time schedule. I worked Tuesdays through Thursdays from 8 to 6, and Mondays, when the shop was closed, I worked for myself from 8 to 6. So I was working four days a week and spent Friday, Saturday and Sunday with my family. What I had accomplished so far in my life had taken a lot of courage, and would not have happened without a positive attitude.

The first step you take is always the most important one…

> *The first few steps you take on any journey*
> *won't get you where you want to go.*
> *But without those first steps*
> *and the many more that follow,*
> *you would always be standing right where you are,*
> *looking towards the future*
> *and wondering what it would really be like to see*
> *your world the way you always dreamed it could be.*
>
> *One of the greatest lessons in life*
> *is the one you learn about moving forward*
> *and taking steps to reach your goals.*
> *Life rewards those who are willing*
> *to be involved in it and take chances.*
> *Take your chance*
> *and take those first few steps,*
> *because a better life is just waiting for you.*

~ Nick Santana

Now, remember what I said about my mom and dad? They were young in spirit, young at heart, and quite intuitive about a young woman's needs for a fulfilling life. They knew it was time for me to find a Mr. Right to help me bring up my children and to fill my needs as a young woman.

The Second Time Around

Sixty or so years ago, there was this wonderful place just outside Palm Springs called the Highland Springs Hotel. They had what was called Singles Weekends for people in their late twenties to late forties. My mom and dad arranged for me to spend the weekend there at their expense so I could get away and meet some new people.

I arrived full of enthusiasm, ready to begin a new chapter in my life. I arrived on a Friday evening and was immediately surrounded by a group of fun, friendly people who were definitely out to have a good time. We ate dinner, and spent the rest of the evening getting to know each other while singing around the piano.

When Saturday morning came around, it was warm and lovely. I dressed accordingly, in an adorable one-piece bathing suit. With suntan lotion and towel in hand, and with the determination to find a man, I made my way to the pool.

But by 4 o'clock that afternoon, I knew I needed a new modus operandi, as I had not spotted any prospects. So I went back to my room, changed into my new tennis outfit, with matching racquet, and headed for the tennis court. My mother had told me, "If all else fails dear, the tennis court will always win out." How right she was!

I'd been sitting by the court for about half an hour, when a very distinguished older gentleman walked over and invited me to play a set. Without a moment's hesitation, I responded, "Thank you so much, but I just finished playing." Actually, I didn't even know how to play tennis, but I knew I looked so cute in my little tennis outfit, that I would attract attention. And that's exactly what happened. The gentleman's name was Walter, and he said five important words I'll never forget: "Let's have some coffee instead."

We went to the only coffee shop near the hotel, which happened to be a Denny's. We started talking at about 5 in the afternoon, and by 2am we were still talking! It was as if I had known Walter my whole life. We practically shared the same story. He was a widower and I was a widow. I had finally found someone who, like me, was looking for not only a partner, but a parent for their children.

It had been a great weekend at Highland Springs, and Walter and I agreed that we would begin seeing each other. Both of us were excited by the prospect of possibly starting a new life together. We planned to introduce each other to our children the following weekend. But first, I had to get back to work.

On the Monday after Highland Springs, my first manicure customer was Irene Dunn, the famous movie actress. Remember, I was the only one working in the shop on Mondays. As I was doing her nails and telling her about my great weekend and the wonderful man I had met, there was a knock on the door. I opened it to find a delivery man carrying a dozen beautiful red roses.

Me with actress Irene Dunne

When I returned with the roses, Irene asked who they were from. I opened the card which read, "To the loveliest lady, with a mortgage, three kids, and a dog, who I want in my future." Wow! That marked the beginning of the next 39 years of my life.

Thus began a romance that resulted in marriage a year and half later and brought two families together. Walter was thirteen years my senior, and had two children – a boy, Howard, and a girl, Michele. And with my three – Michael, Debbie and Ricky – we had our own version of "The Brady Bunch."

When I went to talk with my rabbi about performing the marriage ceremony, he seemed a little concerned. He asked if I realized that between my children and Walter's, I would be raising five kids. I looked at him, smiled, and said, "Dear rabbi, it's only a few more hamburgers." His response was a huge laugh and a big hug, with the comment, "With that attitude, my dear Jackie, you and Walter will have a beautiful life!"

The Goldberg Bunch

So instead of the Brady Bunch, we became known as the Goldberg Bunch. There were two young boys, Richard (mine) and Howard (Walter's), both eight years old; two young girls, Deborah (mine) and Michele (Walter's), both 11 years old; and one older boy, Michael (mine), age 13. In our minds, they all became "ours." It wasn't easy, but life never is. But I can confirm that it was definitely a marriage made in Heaven!

Michael, Debbie and Ricky Penn
children of Jackie Penn
and
Michele and Howard Goldberg
children of Walter Goldberg
request the honour of your presence
at the wedding reception
of their parents

Jackie and Walter

on Sunday, the eighteenth of June
at twelve-thirty o'clock

Tail o' The Cock
477 South La Cienega Boulevard
Los Angeles, California

Let me share a couple of Goldberg Bunch experiences that will surely make you smile – little bits of fun I remember with a shake of my head and a "how did I survive that?"

One experience I will never forget was our family adventure on a houseboat down the Sacramento River with my husband, my parents, five kids, and a 90-pound Old English Sheepdog named Shadow. No one realized this wouldn't be the Grand Hotel. We had allowed the kids to pack their own suitcases, which ended up being filled with clothes they would never wear. My folks thought a houseboat would be similar to a cruise ship, and came on board with enough dressy clothes for two weeks, including my mom's fur coat and wig case, and my dad's tuxedo!

Besides all this, Walter and I had our own suitcases. So now we were on serious overload as we took off down the Sacramento River. Eight hours later, we were beached on a sandbar. The boat was just too heavy! We had no choice but to dump some of the clothes.

Even with all this luggage, no one had thought to bring a flashlight, batteries for the radio, or even an extra blanket. And to make matters worse, it started to rain. Then the electricity on the boat went out. Suddenly, there were no lights, no stove, no refrigerator, and no radio. So we did what any family with a positive attitude would do: We made it work. We drank warm Coke and ate soggy white bread peanut butter and jelly sandwiches. Meanwhile, my mother sat on the deck, wearing her wig and fur coat, with tears in her eyes, lamenting, "If the ship sinks, save the kids first. Dad and I will be fine, we've had a good life." You would have thought we were in the middle of the Pacific Ocean!

Well, we neither sank nor drowned that weekend. But looking back, it was a great experience in communication. Living in such close quarters, we really had the opportunity to get to know and love our family members. By the way, Shadow was the happiest passenger of all. Who knew Old English Sheepdogs loved the rain!

The Goldbergs… so many memories

Another hilarious story involved my two younger boys who were around 13 at the time and first-year students at El Camino High School. They asked if I would help them with one of their school projects. They were assigned to create and cultivate their own garden. Well, of course I would help them. I provided the money for rakes, seeds, shovels, and soil, and they were thrilled. My two very excited boys became the new "Farmers" of Woodland Hills. The effect all of this had on them was miraculous. Their behavior and attitude took a one hundred and eighty degree turn. They did their homework without being asked, and helped around the house without being reminded. It was a fantastic time.

One day, as the garden was thriving so beautifully in my yard, a friend stopped by. Now, this friend happened to be a captain at the local police station. He smiled at me over coffee and asked, "Jackie, do you know what's in your garden?" I replied, "Green plants. I don't know what kind." He suggested I find out.

After visiting my favorite nursery, I did what every red-blooded American mother would do. I immediately went to the high school and asked that my two wonderful boys be excused to come home with me, as we had an emergency. That emergency was their "garden."

I immediately informed them they would have to dig up their garden, and they were horrified. I'm sure you can guess what they were growing. Yep, I had been nurturing the most beautiful, exotic marijuana plants in the San Fernando Valley! With tears in their eyes, they protested, "But Mom, we told all our school friends that we had the coolest mother in the world, because she's letting us grow our plants." Well, their gardening days were now over, and their view of their "cool" mother was shattered. Oh well, that's life!

Five children, five different personalities, and a hundred stories among them.

Walter and me, the happy couple

The "Pink Lady" Is Born

Walter was a very successful women's-wear sales representative. For more than 20 years, he had a showroom at the California Mart in downtown Los Angeles. I started to work with him as soon as we got married. Walter reasoned that with my energy, enthusiasm and attitude, I could be a natural salesperson.

How true that proved to be. Within six months I had helped increase the business by 25%. I loved the excitement of selling to and working with all the different kinds of buyers – small and large – from Judy's and Contempo's to the Mervyn's conglomerate.

In our business, as women's-wear sales reps, travel was a pivotal word. We traveled to San Francisco five times a year, Arizona three times a year, down to the California-Mexico border four times a year, and to Las Vegas once a month. I soon became the "Queen of Vegas."

After only two years of working with Walter, my personality and positive attitude had helped get our merchandise into practically every hotel in Las Vegas and in many theme parks throughout the country. My love for the theatre was still with me. My customers were my audience, and their orders were my applause.

S	M	T	W	T	F	S
1	2	3	4	5	6	7
8	9	10	11	12	13	14
15	16	17	18	19	20	21
22	23	24	25	26	27	28
29	30	31				

Terrific team Walter and Jackie Goldberg of Suite B1224

DYNAMIC DUO

It was a "singles weekend" 21 years ago that brought actress/beautician Jackie and apparel salesman Walter Goldberg of Suite B1224 together. Jackie's thespian nature was evident at their first meeting when, although she sported an expensive tennis dress and racket, she never intended to step onto the court. Both previously widowed, the Goldbergs united their lives—and their children—eight months later.

It was not until Jackie's retail store burned down 6 years ago that she joined Walter's full-time staff in his California Mart Showroom. Of working with her husband Jackie exclaims, "It's invigorating! The people are my favorite aspect of the industry, and Walter lets me be 'the star' while he's 'the backbone' of the business."

Traveling to markets is a frequent adventure for the Goldbergs. Jackie was once offered a job and Walter was mistaken for her boss. Beyond business, most of their travels take them to Palm Springs or visiting their 5 children and 4 grandchildren.

CALENDAR OF EVENTS

MARCH 5 "Increased Profitability Via Electronic Data Link with Major Retailers," seminar sponsored by KMG Main Hurdman and MAI Basic Four, 9:00 a.m., LA Suite, C678

MARCH 16-18 California Mart Petite Market, 9:00 a.m. to 5:00 p.m., Exhibit Hall and participating showrooms

MARCH 16 "Who is the Petite Customer and What are Her Fashion Needs?" seminar and continental breakfast, 8:30 a.m., Fashion Theatre

MARCH 17 Petite Fashion Show and continental breakfast, 8:30 a.m., Galleria

MARCH 18 "Growth in Market Strategies 1987," seminar and continental breakfast, 8:30 a.m., Fashion Theatre

MARCH 21 Consumer Productions Saturday Sale, 10:00 a.m. to 4:00 p.m., Exhibit Hall

The California Mart monthly paper

People always ask when and where the "Pink Lady" persona was born. It happened one day in 1966 at the California Mart. At that time, I would wear all different colors, but I happened to be wearing pink on that particular day. As I walked down the hall near our showroom, someone yelled out, "Hey, Pink Lady." Now, most people would have just let it go, but my husband was a marketing genius. He had heard the gentleman call me Pink Lady, and he asked me, "Would you like to be known throughout our industry?" And I answered, "Of course!" Walter continued, "Okay, from this day forward you will be known as The Pink Lady."

June 28, 2005

Two weeks later, Walter had a massive sign painted on our showroom window that read, "Walter P. Goldberg and Associates, starring…" and inside a huge pink star were the words "The Pink Lady." This was the pivotal moment that would launch the journey of a lifetime for the Pink Lady. The famous (and infamous) image would become my persona and way of life from that moment forward. And here we are 50 years later, and the Pink Lady is still going strong!

I'm convinced that in everyone's life there are moments that make us feel that no matter what happens to us, it's all worthwhile. When I became the Pink Lady, it opened up so many new doors of opportunity. I became one of the most popular and respected salespeople in our business. And in my personal life, I actually lived as the Pink Lady. From my clothes, to my home, to having my grandchildren call me "Pink Grandma," it was the best idea anyone could have come up with. No one whom I have met over the years forgets the Pink Lady. This simple idea, this brand that Walter started more than five decades ago, has carried me through the years and has given me positive notoriety wherever I go and in whatever I do.

And now, at this time in my life, nearly every day, people stop me and ask to take my picture. "We love your pink hair and pink clothes. You are so adorable." I definitely make a statement of who I am wherever I go, and demonstrate that being who you really are can be fun! Such an attitude will keep you continually out there – and actively creative in your own way.

A New Twist in a Perfect World

For 39 wonderful years, with a terrific husband and business partner by my side, we raised our five children and celebrated Bar Mitzvahs for the boys and a fabulous Double Sweet Sixteen Party for the girls, along with my wonderful Mom and Dad who had helped us create a most fulfilling life. With my personal and business life complete, I was at peace. I was the Pink Lady who always had a positive attitude, which allowed me to view life through rose-colored glasses.

Our lifestyle was now set. Business was good and the kids were grown and had started families of their own. Before you knew it, we had six grandchildren! We were happy, we were blessed.

Then suddenly at age 76, Walter began having symptoms of the dreaded Alzheimer's disease. A year later he had to retire, and for the next few years, I ran the business alone. I continued to work at the Mart, traveling to women's- wear trade shows, and doing everything I could to keep my everyday life running as normal as possible.

Soon thereafter, I was working a trade show in Arizona by myself. The show ended at 6pm and I had to be in Las Vegas the next day to start work at 7:30 in the morning. As I was packing up my van, the notorious Arizona rains hit. A few of the other salesmen were quite worried about me going out on the open road, in the rainstorm, by myself. Yes, sometimes my attitude can be a bit stubborn. I thanked them all for their concern, but knew what I had to do and started driving toward Vegas.

Within an hour, the heavens opened up with thunder, lightning and torrential rain. I managed to pull over into a truck stop and went in for a cup of coffee. I guess I must have looked mighty forlorn sitting there at the counter, because one of the truckers approached me and asked if he could help in any way. When I told him I had to be in Vegas in the morning, he looked at me, smiled and acknowledged, "I get it." And, then he did the nicest thing. He offered to escort me to Vegas by having me follow his 18 wheeler, with all its brilliant lights, at the proper speed, which enabled me to arrive at my destination safely and on time.

Some might ask why I would have risked my safety like that. But I knew why; I simply didn't want to disappoint Walter. I ended up getting there, on time, and took care of business like we had always done together before. There have been so many people through the years who have helped me when I've been alone. I guess me being me, and having the type of attitude that I have, has brought out the best in those around me.

Walter passed away in January 2003. Losing your significant other, your partner in life and best friend, is devastating to anyone. When I became a widow for the second time, my friends and family told me to join a support group to be with others who were experiencing the same grief. I must tell you, honestly, support groups did not do it for me. I realize that every one of us is different, but I'm the type of individual who does not do well in a 'down' environment. Not everyone views this type of group in that manner, but hearing the other people's stories and their immense sadness was just too much for me to handle. I felt worse than before, sadder and more alone.

After two or three attempts of trying my best to fit in with the group, I realized I needed a more upbeat, uninhibited environment, where people were looking toward tomorrow rather than dwelling on the past. The leader of the bereavement group told me that "time heals everything" and that it could take a while for me to get back to being myself and feeling better. But knowing my personality and the type of life I had always lived, I knew I needed to fast- forward through this period in order to save my sanity and my life.

I quickly realized that life goes on and that attitudes must continue to be positive. You know, it's perfectly okay to get on with your life and still keep the beautiful memories and experiences alive that you shared with your loved one. Through these memories, you can still be in touch with your past, while simultaneously giving yourself permission to have a future.

I told my children and friends that I would be happy to have them around to help me through this tough time. But I also warned them not to spoil me with kindness. I needed to explore new avenues on my own and meet new people as soon as possible. Being alone and feeling sorry for myself was not going to be an option.

Is life over for a woman who is alone at the age of 71? For me, the choice was simple. I knew I was a survivor and that I could start all over again using the positive attitude that had been such a blessing to me throughout my life.

A year and a half after the loss of my husband, I was still working hard at my sales rep business and traveling to markets in San Francisco, Arizona and even parts of Mexico. I was putting in long hours six and seven days a week. I must tell you that it did help me to overcome my loneliness. It was a crutch for me, and it gave me a great deal to do which left no time for self-pity.

Pink Lady President, Pacific Coast Travelers

As my business continued to grow and require more and more travel, I really needed help in the office; someone to accompany me when I would go to all the different markets – which added up to more than 26 weeks a year! I had a talk with my daughter Michele

48

who, at that time, was the only child of mine working in the garment industry. She was a salesperson for a huge dress company. I asked her to join me as my partner, thus helping me out while securing her financial future.

I remember what Walter had said when he became ill... "My dear Jackie, if anything happens to me, I want you to live life to the fullest, because life belongs to the living." That was the best advice anyone could have given someone in those circumstances. He was a very caring and devoted husband and provider for his family, and truly was my best friend.

Four years into his Alzheimer's, I had hired a live-in caregiver so that I could still work and travel. My older son, Michael, his wife Harumi, her parents, Fusako and Iwao, and grandchildren, Miko and Andrew wanted me to take a trip with them to France. I thought about it and finally said yes, since I hadn't had a vacation in over five years.

So, off to France we went. It was December 1999 and we wanted to be in Paris at the Eiffel Tower for the Millennium. There were seven of us. OMG! What a time we picked to go away! France was experiencing the worst winter in over 100 years. Oh well, "c'est la vie." We went to the south coast first, and were having a great time despite the cold weather. Our plans were to head back to Paris on December 30th by train.

Well, December 30th dawned, and all hell broke loose! Nearly all travel to Paris was suspended due to a monster snow storm that had hit the night before. In fact, there was only one train from the city of Arles, which was where we were staying, scheduled to leave at 9 o'clock that evening.

At noon that day, with the weather dropping below 30 degrees, the seven of us made our way to the train station to get tickets for Paris. When we arrived, we couldn't believe our eyes. There must have been over 500 people waiting in line at the ticket window for the same train. My son said, "Stay put, everyone. I'll get in line for the tickets." Due to the freezing temperature, most of the people were in a truly bad mood. They were hungry, cold and afraid they wouldn't get on the train. I knew at that moment that my son wouldn't be able to get us the tickets we needed. No one was going to allow a 5'10" young man to make his way up to the ticket window from the back of the line.

Just then my attitude button kicked on and I announced to my son, "This crowd is never going to let you get anywhere near that window. But they will let a little old lady with pink sneakers, a pink parka and pink hair push all of her 4'11", 90-pound weight through." Immediately my family began pleading, "No Mom, you'll get hurt!" while Miko and Andrew yelled out "Pink Grandma, they're gonna kill you!" Nevertheless, off I went, ignoring their protests.

I started at the back of the line saying, "Excusez moi. Pardonnez moi. Voulez vous, let me pass?" (My French isn't too good, and I'm so sorry I didn't get a video of this. Talk about attitude in battle!) To my family's complete surprise, people were letting me pass. I think they were in shock that anyone would have the chutzpah to be pushing her way through hundreds of people to get to the ticket window, yelling in pigeon French, "Excusez moi! Stop pushing! Let me by! I'm a little old lady!" And I made it through!

When the ticket office opened, there stood "The Ticket Master from Hell!" I asked for seven sleeper tickets for the 9 o'clock train to Paris, and the woman behind the window said, "Non, non – quatre – four!" And I argued, "No, no – seven!" This exchange went on for at least five minutes, with the crowd behind me getting very angry and more volatile. The ticket master looked at me, looked at the crowd and must have realized that I was not going anywhere without my seven sleeper tickets. And so, grudgingly, she handed them over! Yes, my positive attitude had once again won the battle!

I thank God for this positive perspective! My family and I – all seven of us – got to Paris and celebrated the Millennium year 2000 in front of the Eiffel Tower on December 31st. Who says something *little* can't be mighty? My positive attitude has always given me the strength to find my way at different traumatic times in my life.

When I talk about attitude, I realize that, like a color, it can come in many different shades. But what I'm most sure of is that all of us have what I call a "survival attitude." And so when Walter died, I made it through by taking it step by step. Each one of us has our ups and downs. I'm no different. I have good days and bad days. But it's the way we pick ourselves up and move on that makes all the difference.

Onward and Upward

Entering into the real world alone after being with my husband, who was not only my partner and lover, but my best friend, was a real challenge. Believe me, it took quite a few pink candles, prayers and "I can do this" to take the first step. But the time comes when you just have to begin. And so I started going to the movies alone, dining at restaurants by myself, and then, finally, the big step: attending singles events.

My first event as a single woman was fun, and it was easy, since everyone else was essentially in the same position. I did meet some very nice people and realized that after being married for 39 years, it wasn't really a problem for me to say hello to people I didn't know. But it was up to me to take the first step. It's like a Monopoly game. Begin with step one, *Get Up.* Then go to step two, *Get Out* of the house. And I knew that step three, *Get a Life,* was just around the corner.

Starting a new life after I became a widow took a lot of planning. I had family and friends as a great support system, but I quickly understood that not only did they have their own lives, but that it was important for me as well to have a life of my own.

There are five things I would advise you to do at the outset:

1. *Don't waste time feeling sorry for yourself.*
2. *Don't panic. Most people are kind.*
3. *Be adventurous and take chances.*

4. Give it all you've got and go for broke.
5. Eat, drink and be merry, for tomorrow is another day.

Putting it all together and getting up is not that hard to do. You need to just do it! Realize that by trying a few different options, you will actually gain a new life just by experiencing new situations. There are many single men and women in the over-60 age group who are divorced or who have lost their partners. So the best chance for starting your new life is to meet others at group affairs like sporting events, book clubs, bridge clubs or religious get-togethers.

Courage for a New Life

In order to move on, it takes courage, passion, and an inner conviction that we're doing the right thing. The most important thing is for us to believe in ourselves. It's not easy to begin again. Trust me, I know that for a fact. Our families and friends cannot make a new life happen. You yourself must overcome the biggest obstacle of all, which is the preconceived notion that you cannot begin again. It will never happen without a positive attitude that says we can go in a different direction than the one we've been traveling. You must feel comfortable in your own skin, and be confident in your own special creativity, realizing that you are your own unique person.

We must believe that we can do whatever we set out to do. We need to make that attitude a part of our everyday life. I did it. Now my goal is to help others realize that when they're over 60, or at any age, they're not people who are getting old, but people who are only getting "older." It's true... people are like wine; we get better with age.

After being knocked down by circumstances, if you feel you have to pull yourself out of bed in the morning, pull yourself to work and pull yourself back home again, you're definitely living life the wrong way. Life does require effort to survive, but forcing yourself to live it is not the way to go. In fact, pulling yourself around will send you on a non-productive, negative journey. Instead, we should allow our dreams and goals to gently push and guide us through life.

It's really all about passion and purpose. By changing our way of thinking and focusing on our passions in life, we give ourselves the tools to rise above the hurdles that life puts in our path. We will get where we want to go eventually, but we will each do it in our own unique way and in our own time frame. The ways in which we achieve what we want doesn't matter. What does matter is that we enjoy the journey and not give up on ourselves.

Don't let anything or anyone deter you from reaching your goals. You will succeed in your own good time if you're truly passionate and positive about what you want. Getting up is the hardest part, but it will definitely be worth it.

I won't presume to tell you that it's easy to get up when a tragedy has occurred in your life. The loss of a family member or a dear friend, or even the breakup of a disappointing relationship will affect you physically, mentally and spiritually, but you can do it... I did! I made up my mind to believe Walter when he said, "life is for the living." I made the decision to choose to enjoy the rest of my life. In order for us to start to live again, and to follow new paths, we must look deep inside ourselves and be honest about what we see.

Sometimes it takes a change in attitude in order to move forward. But one also has to feel proud about who they are and to recognize the potential that we each have. We are all vital and valuable human beings. If you combine that insight with a positive attitude, you will accomplish what you've set out to do. You'll understand that the best years of your life are still ahead of you. Thankfully, most of us have family, friends, and significant others to back us up.

Here are a few suggestions to help get you through the first stage of *Getting Up:*

> 1. *Put yourself in the frame of mind of wanting to get up. Forget what was and focus on what can be.*
> 2. *Take a good look at yourself in the mirror. Try to be objective about what you see. If, like many of us at this stage, you see a person who has developed some lines or put on a few pounds, just know that those things can be corrected. Take this opportunity to start a new regimen of getting back into shape. Start watching what you eat and begin an exercise program.*

3. Take a few days to go through your closet. I realize it might take a concerted effort to get rid of some of the clothes you've become attached to, but do it! Get rid of anything that doesn't make you look good. Sometimes – and don't laugh – color can make or break a person's daily outlook. I'm not saying that everyone should wear pink all the time (like me), but I do suggest you find colors that bring out your best and make you feel good.

4. There are always people around who can bring us down if we're not careful. You need positive forces around you at this critical time. Surround yourself with people that make you feel exhilarated to be alive.

5. Realize that getting up is only the first step in moving toward this new phase in your life. I'm not implying it will be easy, but it can be done. I'm not saying that you can do it in a week, a month or six months, but I am telling you that IT CAN BE DONE in order for you to get on with the rest of your life. It is imperative not to waste the fabulous years you have left.

Taking risks and setting goals make life exciting and worthwhile. In order to grow as human beings, we need to experience challenges. Eleanor Roosevelt once said, "Do one thing every day that scares you – embrace the adventure." The best learning happens just beyond our comfort zone. The rewards we receive from taking risks help to spearhead our emotional and spiritual growth. The sense of satisfaction we get from trying something new, and proving to ourselves that we can do it, allows us to enjoy the ride by awakening our senses to exciting new pleasures.

Close your eyes for a moment and think about how wonderful you are. Think about what a special person you are. Say to yourself, "I can be happy with who I am. Given the opportunity, with a positive outlook, I can go wherever, do whatever and be whomever I want to be." When we put on our rose-colored glasses, I believe we can accomplish so much more. We tend to become happier, more vital, and much more creative.

Nothing that's truly worthwhile happens overnight. Whatever is going on, make sure you take the time to smell the roses. Remember, the best medicine for living longer is being able to see the humor in life. Learn to be able to laugh at yourself first, and then you will be able to laugh at the world.

> *This is our time to do what we want, when we want, and how we want. We have earned it, and we deserve it. We have reached the age where we can live our lives our way.*

Cruising with an Attitude

Our experiences, whether good or bad, give us the tools we need to start on the road to recovery and discovery. I knew I wasn't the type of person who could hide from the world. I was always *out there*. I knew I had to *Get Up, Get Out, & Get a Life!* I knew in my heart and mind that I still had places to go, things to do, and people to meet. There was a life out there for me to live, and I intended to do just that – live it! The only way to learn something new is to put yourself out there. It's not a question of "*can* I do something to better my life?" It's really "I *will* do something to better my life!"

I continued working in the garment business for more than two years after Walter passed. During that time I started to ask myself, "Is this all there is?" I was beginning to realize there was more to life than what I was doing. So what do you do when you're 73 years young, newly widowed, with five kids and six grandchildren? It's obvious. You go on a cruise – Alone!

The next thing I had to think about was "who am I?" Being the Pink Lady and being a single woman once again, I knew that if I was going to do something like this, it would have to be for fun and for a new beginning. I decided on a seven-day cruise… not too short, not too long. I wanted an itinerary that would include air travel, going on excursions and the experience of going through customs. So I chose a Princess Cruise to the Caribbean. I knew I wasn't 30 or 40 anymore. But I also knew that even in my 70s, I could still have fun and open myself up to making new friends and relationships. I was so excited!

I started laying out my clothes weeks in advance. I soon realized that I would need three steamer trunks to fit everything in. Not a good sign. It wasn't as though I had a lot of color choices to make, since everything I owned, naturally, was pink! So I began to re-pack, and eventually got it down to two large suitcases and a carry-on.

The day of my trip arrived, and I looked great! Hair, makeup, outfit... all cruise ready. I landed in Miami at 10am, caught a glimpse of myself in the mirror at 11 and started to cry. My beautiful curly hair was now straight as sticks. The curse of humidity!

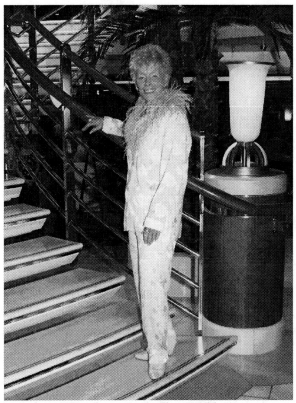

My solo cruise to the Caribbean

So what does a smart, single California woman do in a situation like this? She buys a pack of curlers, three hats, five scarves, and lots of hair spray. Nothing was going to stop me from looking fabulous and having a great time. I knew that boarding time would be the moment of reckoning for me. It would either make or break my experience aboard the ship.

When I arrived at the boarding dock, they asked me my name. I knew then and there what my answer had to be. Loud and clear, with two or three hundred people within earshot in line behind me, I proudly announced, "I am the Pink Lady." The steward at the desk looked at me, asked for my ID (which had my legal name on it), and responded, "Thank you, Pink Lady." By the time I had walked up the gangplank, the on-board crew greeted me with a cheerful "Welcome aboard Princess Cruises, Pink Lady." I knew right then that I was going to have the time of my life... and I did!

Here are a couple of helpful hints for single people on cruises. The first thing I did after unpacking was go to the dining room and find the maître d'. I slipped him a ten-dollar bill (today it would have to be fifty) and asked him to put me at a table for ten. I knew that being at one table with a lot of other people was the key to helping me network at the very first meal and start the cruise off on a positive note.

The second hint: Find the activities director and let him or her know that you're always available and ready to have a good time. Because I did that, and because of my outgoing attitude, I was included in most of the activities throughout the cruise. Now, not everyone is as outgoing as I am, but you should at least try to put yourself out there in order to maximize your chances to have fun and meet new people.

The second night out was the Captain's Dinner, and I was dressed in a fabulous pink outfit. (What else would you expect?) I had a few moments to kill before dinner, so I stopped by the ship's boutique. As I was turning to leave, a drop-dead-gorgeous, six-foot- plus gentleman in uniform said, "Good evening." And I countered, "Good evening. I'm the Pink Lady," Whereupon he smiled and proclaimed, "My dear, I know who you are. The whole ship is talking about the lovely Pink Lady." Yes, it was the captain, and he invited me to sit at the captain's table that evening, as well as the next two nights after that!

Talk about attitude! I realized I had to be *out there*. I went on all the land tours, participated in all the activities, and made a place for myself in the world – alone, but not really alone. For I was making some lovely new friends on that cruise, many of whom remain friends to this day. Once again, I realized that I was not the type of person who wanted to hide from the world. I wanted to be in the world – enjoying it all.

It sounds like it was easy for me. Not true! When I announced my name at the check-in desk at the dock, I was apprehensive. But I knew that I had to either do it all the way or not do it at all. I want everyone to know that being who you are is what's going to carry you through anything and everything that you will encounter in life. Having the attitude that you're special, and that you deserve to have everything you want in life, helps you to deal with the difficult times that will come your way.

Although a cruise may not be how you choose to deal with a loss, make sure that the first steps you do take, bring you back to life, surrounded by family, friends and, hopefully, new and interesting people. Once I arrived home, I knew I was ready to be the Pink Lady – a woman *on her own, with an attitude!*

Aging with an Attitude

I think this cute little story says it all about the process of aging with the right attitude: Three elderly ladies were talking about what they hoped their grandchildren would be saying about them 50 years from now. The first lady declared, "I would like my grandchildren to say that she was successful in business." The second one offered, "I want them to say that she was a loyal family member." Turning to the third lady, "So what do you want your grandchildren to say about you in 50 years?" She replied, "That's easy, I want them to all say she certainly looked good for her age."

Attitude. It can begin at any moment – anywhere, and in a thousand different ways. What enables each of us to accomplish the things we want to do? What makes me, at this wondrous time in my life, able to help others see that life is not over, but simply out there for the taking? My dear friends, it's attitude. You can't fake it – you can't turn it on or off – you just have to feel it, breathe it, and live it!

Attitudes can make or break almost everything we do. Every day we have choices to make regarding our attitude. We cannot change our past or change the inevitable, but I'm convinced that we can change the way we live our lives. The longer I live, the more I realize the impact of attitude. It can determine the course of any situation we are in or any goal that we are trying to achieve.

I have a wonderful philosophy about living my life in a positive way. My philosophy, of course, is "to *think pink*; to feel the energy and the aura of beauty that a color can give by letting people see life through rose-colored glasses. It makes living, loving, and laughing a beautiful way of life. Whoever comes in contact with this color shares my philosophy, which is "to see love and inner beauty in everything and everyone around them. It has given me a chance to share this passion with my family, my friends, and my community, hopefully making this world a better place in the process."

I speak to you from my heart when I say that I truly believe in this philosophy. It can apply to anyone, no matter what your favorite color is. Your positive attitude will shine through. Whatever your favorite color is, make sure it enables you to create the world in which you truly want to live.

People today are not following the tradition of retiring at age 55 or 65. Instead, they're reinventing themselves by moving into second and third careers. Life can still be exciting and adventurous during this period. I reinvented myself into three new careers while in my 70s. I became an actress, a motivational speaker, and the founder of Senior Star Power Productions, a 501(c)(3) not-for-profit corporation whose mission is to engage, inspire and enrich the lives of seniors and veterans through the arts. My goal with Senior Star Power is to have a year round Senior Theatrical Arts Complex. With the right attitude, I believe it's possible to accomplish anything, including achieving my dream of having my own theater.

If you're not satisfied with where you are, you need to change your outlook on how you're living and redefine yourself so you can continue to grow. Simply put, when you stop growing, you stop living. You are the master of your own emotions. The only person who can change or control the way you feel about yourself is you!

Living life to the max has a lot to do with our ability to be flexible and creative in our lifestyle and our relationships. If we utilize past experiences, good or bad, and balance them with new and fabulous adventures, we will be able to make our senior years not only joyous, but worthwhile and exciting.

My mantra is "I can and will succeed in whatever I set out to do. I will use my body, my soul, and my life experiences to get the most out of these beautiful and wondrous years of my life... now... today... and at this very moment."

Getting an "Attitude" Adjustment

This is a wonderful world we live in. And it's an extraordinary time to be able to live the life we've always wanted. When we are positive, we feel empowered to do our very best. No matter what age we are, each of us wants to be happy and satisfied with our life. Today's world is definitely not as easy as the movies make it seem. At times it takes more than attitude to solve a problem. But having the right attitude makes it "a hell of a lot easier" to accomplish what needs to be done.

A while back in my travels, I happened upon a quirky establishment that made my day. It was called the Attitude Adjustment Shoppe. My dream would be to send anyone who needs a little help in getting a more positive attitude to this store for a few lessons. Wouldn't that be a delightful and easy way to make everyone happy?

The scientific community has found, through years of research, that keeping our minds engaged in a positive state can stave off physical and mental ailments. Positive attitudes are known to help the "mature adult" generation live longer and more productive lives. Keeping our brains active by learning new skills, taking classes, and involving ourselves in community volunteer activities is turning our generation around. We're not just sitting in rocking chairs. We are active, engaged, and out there creating new lifestyles as we move into our 60 plus years.

Being young at heart makes one feel that every door of life is still wide open, and that anything and everything is possible and within our reach. That key ingredient – a positive attitude – has given me the desire to accomplish new and exciting things that can only come about when you have the motivation and determination to reach for the stars and catch them. Enjoy the simple things in life. Take nothing for granted. Laugh and love through all of life's changes.

We know that time is not on our side. As we age, the time we take to enjoy the things we never did in the past becomes even more precious. I believe that our lives grow richer as we grow older, because we realize just how dear our time on Earth truly is. We also find that our spiritual side grows stronger with age. We need to be in tune with the Universe. I believe the Universe gives out a certain type of energy that will help us find the inner strength we need to continue moving our lives on the right path. And remember to thank God for giving you each new day to enjoy who you are – a remarkable human being.

Getting older does not mean growing old, and it certainly does not equate with giving up on life. It takes a bit of adjustment in our own minds to acknowledge that as we age, there will be normal limitations that come into play. But the right attitude can help us deal with appearance changes that naturally occur. We can also adjust to the loss of some physical strength by learning new ways to continue to do the things we've always enjoyed doing.

We can make sure, by having a positive attitude, that we never lose our sense of humor. Being able to laugh at ourselves and have fun can make a big difference in enjoying the rest of our lives. I love this quote: "What good does it do us to add years to our lives if, at the same time, we do not add life to our years?"

The best part of aging, I believe, is that we become more creative. This is a result of our accumulated experiences. We learn that even though we can't do anything about the aging process, we can still pursue a positive lifestyle by learning from the past, correcting our mistakes, and living the rest of our lives in a more productive way.

At this stage, we have control over most areas of our lives. We're at a point where we only have to answer to ourselves. We don't have to prove who we are. We should *know* who we are.

1. The years from 0 to 25, I call the me/myself years.
2. The years from 26 to 59, I call the family years.
3. The years from 60 on are the best years! These are the ones that will mean the most to us. There's no need to mourn the past or worry about the future, but to live in the present – wisely, earnestly, and lovingly, with the right attitude to enjoy it all.

Get over being unhappy or unsatisfied with who you are – for you are you. Realize that you are unique – there is no one like you in the whole world. And it's never too late to reinvent that uniqueness in order to find a more exciting new way of life. All it takes to succeed is determination and a commitment to accomplish the goals you set for yourself.

I'm so blessed and happy to be who I am. You should all feel the same way about yourselves. The number one key to longevity is a happy attitude. In all honesty, when I was thrown against a brick wall, I used my positive attitude to find a gate I could go through in order to continue my life in a positive way. I believe everyone has the potential to have the same energy and zest for life that I have. My children and grandchildren have said over and over again that if they could bottle my energy and enthusiasm and sell it, they would become instant millionaires. You just have to learn how to access your own energy and release it into the Universe to achieve what you want.

There are days when all of us wonder, "Can I really get up and change my life?" You will find the strength to change it if you want to badly enough. You will find yourself overcoming obstacles that you thought you never could. You just have to make sure that you have those positive thoughts on your side. Every one of us can make a difference every day in our own lives and in those around us. We have the power to change not just our lives, but the world!

When we understand that growing older is normal, and adjust our attitudes to make the time we have here on Earth more productive, we will then have a chance to live more creative, viable lives. When we are energized, enthusiastic and excited, it becomes contagious to everyone around us.

Sometimes, all we have to do is remind ourselves how lucky we are to be here. Having an attitude adjustment when we're feeling down, or when things aren't going the way we want them to, should help remind us that no matter what happens, we can still get up and live, love and laugh our way through it all.

I believe that everyone has the power to create the energy that will help them get enthusiastic and passionate enough to reach the goals they set for themselves. It takes an inner voice with conviction that says, "Yes, you can accomplish what you're setting out to do." Happiness does not depend on what happens outside of you, but what happens on the inside. It is measured by the spirit with which you meet the problems that life deals you. This is your time to live your life the way you want to – not the way someone else wants you to.

Raise your expectations of what is truly possible for you to accomplish. If you really desire that new, exciting life, you must open your mind to all the possibilities before you. You must be motivated mentally, physically, and spiritually. By continuing to get up, you will ease into a new way of life, both enjoyable and comfortable.

Everyday is a new day, and the first day of the rest of your life. It's a wonderful gift, so why not enjoy it. Each morning you should start your day with these words: "I BELIEVE WITH ALL MY HEART AND SOUL THAT I CAN AND WILL SUCCEED IN WHATEVER I SET OUT TO DO!"

Section Two
GET OUT – Learn to Live Longer, Better, and Wiser

Moving On

Having been a salesperson for over 40 years, the idea of starting a new career was a bit daunting. What did I really want to do? I knew that to reinvent myself I'd have to think of something that would lead me into meeting new people and be fun and exciting at the same time.

So I tried a few different avenues to see where I wanted to go on my journey of self-reinvention. It just happened that a friend who had started classes on becoming a hypnotherapist told me what a good teacher she was studying with. Her name was Shelly Stockwell Nichols, a world-renowned hypnotist.

The idea of helping people appealed to me, and I thought this would be a good way to help myself at the same time. I took Shelly's course and enjoyed every minute of it. My friend was right! Shelly knew everything about her craft and had a delightful and energetic way of teaching us what we needed to know.

Inside of a few months, I started to practice hypnotherapy by working on my fellow classmates. What an eye-opening experience that was! I found myself fascinated by how people's minds and emotions were all so very different. I soon learned that to be an effective hypnotherapist would take many years of study and practice. I decided after taking classes for about six months that I was not ready to devote the rest of my life to this vocation. It is a fabulous tool for helping people, and I did learn many helpful hints that I use to this day in my seminars, but it wasn't for me. Even so, the International Hypnosis Federation saw fit to give me the Humanitarian Award in 2012 because of the work I had done in helping others.

Welcome to The International Hypnosis Federation
Saturday, March 3, 2012, 7-10 pm BANQUET/SHOW
DoubleTree by Hilton Hotel, San Pedro

6:30 pm
No Host
Bar

AWARDS BANQUET SHOW

7pm Invocation: Jim Hale on the trumpet
Shelley Stockwell-Nicholas Master of Ceramonies
and Susan Picking Song Weaver

DR NEVE'S CHAIRMAN'S
RECOGNITION AWARD
Suzy Prudden Raffle Queen
Prizes from our wonderful members/vendors
& 50/50 CASH Raffle

2012 HUMANITARIAN
JACQUELINE GOLDBERG
"PINK LADY"

Arnold Arch Introduction
"ROCKIN' With The Ages"

Tribute: Carole Woodbury, Valerie
Paradise Lant, Sue Smart, Phyllis Lovit

Pink Lady: "Get Up Get Out
And Get A Life"

Menu
* vegetarians show your card/badge for
the chef's choice vegetarian meal.

Caesar Salad
Rolls and Butter
Grilled Salmon with Lemon Butter
Oven Roasted Potatoes
Seasonal Vegetables
Chocolate Decadent Round
Starbucks Coffee, Hot Tea, Iced Water

THANK YOU to our Presenters, Volunteers, Advisory Board and YOU for joining in the fun
IHF Advisory Board! Beverley Bley, CHt, Jaime Feldman, PhD, Helene Feldman, PhD, Frank Genco, CHt, Jillian LaVelle, CHt, Ormond McGill, PhD,
Richard Neves, PhD, Jon Nicholas, CHt, Suzy Prudden, CHt, Shelley Stockwell-Nicholas, PhD, Niccolous Thompson, CHt,
Judy Umansky, CHt, James Wanless, PhD, Michael Almaraz, Michael Holt, Rhona Jordan, CHt

The next step on my journey of *Getting Out* was to take some general classes at UCLA and Pierce College. I am an advocate of education and have always believed that whatever we learn that's new can only benefit us and help us to become more interesting people. Through these classes, I was able to gain more insights and knowledge which would eventually help me in my future acting career, as well as my *Get Up, Get Out, & Get a Life!* seminars.

Life Is For the Living

Look, I'll just say it... one day we are all going to pass away. So, the question isn't whether or not we will die, but how we are going to live! The purpose of life is to live it, to taste its experiences to their fullest, to reach out eagerly and without fear for newer and richer adventures in this joyous journey. Using a positive attitude as our number one tool, our goal is to check out the different avenues that are open to us, and to find interesting and challenging ways to make this new life exciting and worthwhile.

Beware of the way people use the word "still" in their conversations with you. It makes me angry when others ask, "Are you still working?" "Are you still traveling?" "Are you still dating?" Make sure your answer is, "You have got to be kidding! Of course I am! Just because I'm over 60, doesn't mean that I'm dead!" Incidentally, we are still the real backbone of this nation, which is a positive use of the word "still." We are educated, respected, and "still" filled with massive energy and enthusiasm. I believe our nation would benefit and grow much stronger if our country would only tap into the ever growing senior population.

Hooray for us! Let's dream the possible dream, for we can *Get Out* and accomplish whatever we choose to do. The tragedy in life isn't being unable to reach your goals, it's having no goals to reach. There are plenty of internet sites, books and DVDs dealing with keeping active, healthy, and motivated. I realize that at this juncture in our lives, we may have some health issues, and that's to be expected, but there are many ways to improve our lifestyles nonetheless.

Start with body language. First thing – put a smile on your face, pull your shoulders back, and walk proud. Make eye contact with people as if you're really enjoying the life you're living. And in no time, you will! We have five seconds to make an impression on someone. Our posture and our tone of voice have a big impact on that impression. Remember to put the three "E's" back in your life: ENTHUSIASM, EXCITEMENT, and ENERGY. It will make all the difference in how you live the rest of your life. In order to change the world around us, we must first change ourselves.

Whenever I speak to an audience, the first thing I do is say to everyone, "Yes, you are actually seeing me at this moment in "living color." I am definitely "in the pink," from the bottom of my pink toes to the top of my pink hair. I do not just like the color pink, I LOVE the color pink! And I AM PROUD TO BE THE PINK LADY, JACKIE GOLDBERG!

We must learn to take action. Instead of saying, "Maybe it will happen someday," we should take positive steps to get what we want now! Don't procrastinate. Try shifting your perspective of the world to one that's full of potential. This takes discipline and practice, since many of us are used to negatives, not positives. We simply must learn to put ourselves into the right frame of mind to see just how lucky we are with what we already have, and not dwell on what we don't have.

In everything we do, feeling good about ourselves and having high self- esteem will make the difference between success and failure in achieving your goals. We must also learn to have self-control and self-regulation in order to improve our lives. To persevere and set goals without having a sense of self-esteem will not get us anywhere. If we don't have the right attitude, passion, and enthusiasm, we won't get to the next step of *Getting Out* and enjoying life.

Let's take advantage of all that's out there, which I call *the stuff of life*. It will keep us young at heart, regardless of the circumstances we find ourselves in. Like they say, "Don't sweat the small stuff." By *Getting Out*, we have the opportunity to take advantage of everything that is offered to us. By just exercising our brains, keeping our bodies healthy, and making sure our attitudes stay positive, we will remain active and engaged. For our age bracket, *any* movement is better than *no* movement at all. The real key to living longer is to keep busy. Trust me, we can shake, rattle, and roll with the best of them!

When I found myself alone again in my 70s, in my heart and in my mind, I knew there were still places to see, things to do, and people to meet. "There is," I thought, "a life out there for me to live." And it was my intention to do just that... Live it! AND I DID!

The only way to learn something is by putting yourself out there. It's not "Can I do something?" It's "Will I do something to better my life?" I've always been the kind of person who needed to be active and engaged when it came to everyday living. I knew instinctively that being positive and grateful would keep me alive and well.

There isn't a person who doesn't want to make changes at some time in their life. Everyone has something they want to improve on, whether it's giving up a bad habit, making more money, being physically fit, or finding new ways to enjoy a relationship. There's always room to grow, and age has nothing to do with it. The power to accomplish these things is within all of us, no matter what age we are.

In using what I call the "attitude keys on living life," you can become the person you've always wanted to be by:

1. *Believing in your own inner beauty and spirit.*
2. *Following your dreams, discovering your truths.*
3. *Developing your own personality, look, and style.*
4. *Finding your own rules by trusting your feelings and intuition.*
5. *Singing your own song and dancing to your own music.*

The real question is… are you willing to change? Are you ready to start on a new journey? Make sure you have your attitude in place. Because then you can *Get Up, Get Out, & Get a Life!* We are a part of what I call *the ageless generation.* For it's not *what* you do in life, but *how* you do it that determines whether you're fulfilling your destiny. You should be ready, at this very moment in time, to live longer and better.

Get Ready, Get Set, Get Out

Here are a few things you can do as you prepare to *Get Out:*

1. Realize that YOU are the main character in your life story. You must take responsibility for whatever you do.

2. You must stay in the moment. Though it's alright to think about your future and all the things you want to accomplish, it's most important to remain focused on how you'll get to where you want to go. Take it step by step, and enjoy the adventures along the way.

3. Make sure you're honest with yourself, and respectful to who you are at all times.

4. When you realize that you're a unique and beautiful person inside and out, you will love who you are. I've heard it said, "Love yourself first, and you will find love everywhere else."

5. You must have positive, NOT negative, forces around you. Start this process by getting rid of anyone or anything that will take you down as you start to Get Out and find your new life. Only you will know what will make you happy, and you need to make Getting Up and Getting Out an exciting and exhilarating experience.

Think Positive – Go For It!

There are a couple of steps to help you get through the first stages of *Getting Out* and getting going in the right direction.

First, put yourself in the frame of mind to *want* to *Get Out*. Forget what *was*, and concentrate on what *can be*. Perhaps you have led a life that hasn't been all that exciting. You can now look forward to doing things which will be more fulfilling and exhilarating.

Second, as I said, look at yourself in a mirror and try to be objective about what you see. If you see some things that need attention, take heed and change your mindset to fix them as soon as possible. I know it's not always easy to change one's persona, but in many cases, it's something that needs to be changed in order to achieve a more positive outlook.

Norman Vincent Peale gave us one of America's most inspirational poems. He wrote:

Today let's fall in love with the person in the mirror, the one you see every day but seldom truly look at, the one who gives more than he/she ever takes.

Today let's take nothing, not this day, not this moment, not this chance, not even ourselves, for granted. Let's first love who we are.

If you want to get somewhere, you have to know where you want to go and how to get there. Then never, never, never give up.

The secret of life isn't in what happens to you, but what you do with what happens to you.

Help other people to cope with their problems, and your own will be easier to cope with.

Never use the word impossible seriously again. Toss it into the verbal waste bucket. Self-trust is the first secret of success. So believe in and trust yourself.

Stand up to your obstacles and do something about them. You will find that they haven't half the strength you think they have.

Joy increases as you give it, and diminishes as you try to keep it for yourself. In giving it, you will accumulate a deposit of joy greater than you ever believed possible.

How you think about a problem is more important than the problem itself, so always think positively. Go at life with abandon; give it all you've got. And life will give all it has to you.

Your mind will take you far, but it's your heart and your positive attitude that will make things happen. I've said this before, and I'll say it again: "Bottom line is, I'm not buying into the concept that "It's over." I intend to age with grace, dignity, and a divine spirit. I will NOT back down for anyone or anything, for I am who I am and proud of it!"

There is a beauty to having wisdom and experience. Remember, being mature doesn't mean we're old. It means that we're wiser. Martha Graham, when she was 78, proclaimed, "Age is the acceptance of a term of years, but maturity is the glory of years."

You can, should, and must seize the day and make time for yourself to live out your dreams. You deserve to have this part of your life be a beautiful and fantastic experience, full of all kinds of passion and excitement.

Being aware of where you are at this point is very important to your physical, mental, and spiritual well-being. By taking one breath at a time and one moment at a time, you are able to see, hear, and do the things that make you feel good and allow you to realize just how special life really is. You are here only once. But once is enough if you're able to succeed in making your years productive and rewarding.

Blueprint for Happiness:
Building Blocks for Getting Out

Life can be compared in many ways to a mystery novel. It's filled with intrigue, drama, and suspense, and no one knows the ending until it happens.

When my husband Walter died, I didn't know what the rest of my life would be like. The only thing I did know was that I was blessed with five wonderful children, six fantastic grandchildren, and a family that was behind me in whatever I decided to do. So I needed to start thinking about how I would go about creating the next 25 years. And I knew I needed a blueprint to help me find a plan of action.

A blueprint is the beginning stage of building something. Everyone should have a blueprint for their life – just like we have for buildings. The building blocks needed for a wonderful life are *live, love,* and *laugh.* Armed with these three words, every day can be an exciting adventure, full of fun, passion, and enriching experiences which promote harmony and stability. To build any kind of a life, one must learn to meet all of its challenges head on and be ready to handle whatever happens.

You've all heard the lyrics to the song "If I were a Rich Man." Many believe that wealth brings happiness. But if you really live, if you can truly love, and above all, if you can laugh at what life brings your way, you will have all the riches you need. Depending on one's abilities and desires, these three building blocks may be different for each of us, but they will continually teach valuable lessons. Let's look at them individually and see how we can each draft our own blueprint:

LIVE – Live your life with passion and a strong determination to succeed in your goals. You must live life to the fullest by facing it straight on. Don't dodge anything, for you can only gain strength by learning how to cope with what life throws your way. Look your life straight in the eye as if it were a phenomenal novel by making every chapter a learning experience. Life is a continual struggle – a battle which you can win or lose depending on the choices you make. These choices differ for each of us. Life is a precious and wonderful commodity. There's no need to waste your time on any negative thoughts. Instead, draw a blueprint that lets you dive right into the heart of life and feel its pulsating excitement.

LOVE – Remember the song *What the World Needs Now is Love, Sweet Love*? It's a lovely song with a powerful message. It takes many different kinds of love to make the world go 'round. There's a mother's love, a child's love, a grandparent's love, a lover's love, a friend's love, love for a pet – all different, and yet, all the same. The beauty of love is that it allows us care about someone else unconditionally – no holds barred.

LAUGH – the final word in my blueprint. We all know that life is a mixture of comedy and sadness. Laughter is a medicine that all of us should be taking in large doses everyday of our lives. As the saying goes, "Cry and you cry alone, but laugh and the whole world laughs with you." Believe me, nothing is sadder than someone who is unable to laugh at his or her own situation in life. Being happy and able to laugh at our everyday trials and tribulations, at any age, will give us a sense of physical, mental and spiritual well-being. Thus, a funny moment or a humorous story not only makes us laugh, but helps make life for us and those around us richer and more meaningful.

People often ask, "Does humor really heal? Does it really help?" Here's one example that occurred at the funeral of my late husband, Walter. Out of the crowd of friends and family, a woman approached me with a very stern look on her face and complained, "Today's your husband's funeral. Why would you wear that color? You should be ashamed!" As you might guess, she was referring to the fact that I was dressed in pink instead of black. I looked at her with a smile on my face, and without the slightest hesitation replied "I was married to Walter for 39 years. If I didn't wear pink today, he would never recognize me." I walked away thinking to myself that no matter the situation, there will always be *people who don't get it*. I believe a dash of humor will help you through those rough moments.

You don't stop laughing because you grow old. You grow old because you stop laughing.

Life is a wonderful experience, and with a blueprint ready to go, we can use every single second of it to our advantage. We should be grateful just to be here... now... with the ability to grow older with our friends and family (children, grandchildren, great grandchildren). Part of *Getting Up and Getting Out* is learning to live again by opening new doors and finding exciting adventures and beautiful relationships. I believe the best investment you will ever make in your whole life is investing in yourself – at this time in your life.

Negative to Positive Communication

To begin the process of reinventing ourselves and *Getting Out*, we must learn to communicate with others. Active living has proven to be the key to successful aging. Don't listen to those who say, "Why are you doing this or that at your age?" or "You're too old to take up skydiving?" or "Why on earth would you spend time volunteering when you could simply relax and play bridge?" We need to adopt a "use it or lose it" attitude – and must not listen to people who are stagnant who wish to put a negative vibe into the way we want to enjoy our lives. A good example of this is

Grandma Moses who, against all odds, took up painting in her late 70s and continued until she was 101!

A combination of mental stimulation, social connection, and physical challenge provides the perfect ingredients for aging successfully. Taking on new projects at any age stimulates our lives and helps us growing older, not old. People who remain physically, mentally, and socially active can maintain a better and healthier lifestyle well into their 80s, 90s, and beyond!

We all go through traumatic experiences. There are certain losses that you may never get past – like the loss of a loved one, a divorce, or the end of a career. You have to just learn to go around them. Make sure you trust yourself enough to deal with these experiences, and then move on to enjoy the rest of your life. You must learn to incorporate these losses into who you are at this moment, and to weave these experiences into the life you will be living. The biggest mistake you can make is to not *Get Up and Get Out.*

Here are a few simple things you can do to turn negatives into positives:

1. Think about what you want to achieve. Get out of the house, walk, or take up a sport. Do anything to keep moving and busy.
2. If don't already have a pet, you might want to get one. Coming home to an empty house is a very lonely feeling. Having a "friend" who doesn't ask much of you, but gives you unconditional love, is very important.

3. Learning to go to the movies or restaurants alone is not that hard. In fact, it sometimes gives you the space you need before you're ready to meet new people.

4. Family, friends, and co-workers will want to smother you with love, but you must learn to stand on your own. This is a good time to start that project that's been on hold for many years, such as voice lessons, acting, art or dance classes, college courses – things you've always wanted to do but never had the time for – until now.

5. Of course, the best way to survive a loss of any kind is to help someone else. Volunteer at a hospital, a senior center, a museum, a school, or a veterans' home. Helping others is the best way to help yourself.

6. Don't compare your life to others. You have no idea what their journey is all about.

7. Renew and deepen your spiritual faith.

8. Explore your inner adventurer – try things that are new and exciting like the internet, an iPod, a smart phone, Kindle, or Facebook. These will connect you to the social media world.

9. Your limitations are not flaws. Accept yourself as you are – be your own best friend and congratulate yourself for all the good things you do.

10. Just know that the best is yet to come. The most motivating thoughts come from your gratitude for being alive and your ability to Get Up and Get Out to experience the world through rose-colored glasses.

Raise your sights to all things that are possible for you to accomplish. Open yourself up to traveling new roads and have the courage to follow your instincts. We really have so much to be grateful for at this point in our lives. The most obvious is that we're still here, alive and kicking. So let's live this day, this week, this month, and this year as if it were a gift. Start to write your memoirs even if, like me, you've never written anything before. Make the most of a truly natural treasure: YOU!

Remember, it's never too late to change the life you have. It's fun to be your own person and to create your own style. So say goodbye to things that are negative, and say hello to the positive thoughts that will make it easier to *Get Up and Get Out*. The equation for turning positive ideas into dynamic achievements should read:

Attitude + Positive Energy - Negative Thoughts = Accomplished Goals

You can choose the end of your story by what you decide to do or not do at this point in your life. It's really all about how you see yourself. If I were to ask you, "Which of you sees yourself as smart, enthusiastic, and full of fun and energy?" I would hope that everyone of you would raise your hand (just raise one hand, otherwise you'll drop this book).

We all need to live one day at a time. Appreciate the fact that you're slowly but surely attaining the goals that you want for your new life. Communicating with family, friends, associates at work, and the general public needs to be on a positive level. Keep your eye on the road ahead. But never forget those past experiences and treasured memories that brought you to this point.

Those memories can be put to good use in building new and exciting adventures on your journey. If you have the spirit, the courage, and the energy to want to succeed, you'll succeed in achieving that positive new life by building onto the one you've always had. All you'll need to do is refresh, re-examine, and regenerate.

To succeed, you have to take risks. You have to be able to take rejection and face some failure. "Coulda, woulda, shoulda" – erase these words NOW from your mind. Instead, replace them with words such as I CAN – I WANT – I WILL.

Repeat after me: "THIS IS THE LIFE I AM DYING TO LIVE!"

I believe the best investment you will ever make is to invest in yourself. You can start by mentally trashing old guilts and failures. We're all given the same number of hours in a day. Doing what makes us happy and more productive during those hours should be our number one priority.

Finish every day and be done with it. You have done what you could. Some blunders and absurdities no doubt crept in; forget them as soon as you can. Tomorrow is a new day; begin it well and serenely, and with too high a spirit to be cumbered with your old nonsense. This day is all that is good and fair. It is too dear, with its hopes and invitations, to waste a moment on yesterdays.
~ Ralph Waldo Emerson

I'd like to relate a story someone told me that I'll never forget. One evening an old Native American chief from the Cherokee Nation told his grandson about a battle that goes on inside people. "My son," he began, "there is a battle between two wolves inside us all. One is evil. It is filled with anger, envy, greed, arrogance, self-pity, guilt, resentment, and lies. The other is good, filled with joy, love, hope, serenity, humility, kindness, generosity, truth, and compassion." The boy thought about it for a moment, then asked his grandfather, "Which wolf wins the battle?" The old chief simply replied, "The one you feed."

I believe everyone should take the time to write down all their positive traits. Then, on another page, make a list of all your weaknesses. Believe me, you'll be surprised to see how many solid strengths you have compared to your weaknesses. If you add together all of these positive things about yourself, you'll be surprised to discover that you have plenty of ammunition to *Get Out* and make a new life for yourself.

The art of communication should be a wonderful, fun-filled, learning experience. It's not hard if we use the right tone of voice and are able to look people straight in the eye when we speak. Effective communicating involves really listening to the other person. The following steps are helpful to use as we begin to *Get Out* and communicate with new people and encounter new situations:

1. Be yourself no matter what you're discussing. Speak from your heart and organize your thoughts by planning ahead what you want to inform, suggest, or teach the other person.
2. Remember the old adage "You never get a second chance to make a first impression." Make sure your tone of voice is confident and full of energy. Speak "to" a person and not "at" them.
3. Body language is important for good and effective communication. Carry yourself with pride. "Walk into a room as if you own it, and you will."

I got the cutest email the other day from a male friend. It was all about communication with the opposite sex, and it listed the five words women use most when talking with their significant others...

*1) **Fine:** Women use this word to end an argument. It means they are right and you need to keep quiet.*
*2) **Nothing:** This is the calm before the storm. In reality, this means something and you should be on your toes. Arguments that begin with "nothing" usually end in "fine."*
*3) **Go ahead:** This is a dare. This is not permission to actually go ahead and do what you were planning. The correct response is DON'T DO IT!*
*4) **That's OK:** One of the most dangerous statements a woman can make to a man. She's actually saying you need to think long and hard before deciding how you will pay for your mistake.*
*5) **Whatever:** This is a woman's way of saying DROP DEAD!*

Communication can be funny. It's all in the way one expresses oneself. For instance:

A doctor and his wife are having a fight at the breakfast table. The doctor gets up in a rage and finishes the conversation by saying, "And you're not that good in bed either!" and storms out of the house. After some time he realizes that was a rather nasty thing to say, so he calls up his wife. Following MANY rings, she finally answers the phone, and the irritated husband grumbles, "What took you so long to answer the phone?" "I was in bed," she replies. "In bed, this early?" he asks. "Doing what?" She reveals, "Getting a second opinion."

It doesn't matter what age we are, communication is at the heart of everything we do. At any age, at any time, at any place, the way we interact with other people can make or break any situation we're in. Learn to respect others and try to understand where they're coming from, and it will make *Getting Out* that much easier. One of the easiest and most gratifying ways to do this is by volunteering.

Volunteer – Help Yourself by Helping Others

I realized early on that the best medicine for a person's loss is to immerse oneself in as many projects as possible. I knew in my heart and mind that there were still places to see, things to do, and people to meet.

I started to join clubs and became a volunteer for a few organizations. Volunteering seemed to be the best and easiest way to get myself back out into the world. Utilizing my past experiences and positive attitude, I felt I could be of help to others. I carefully chose where I wanted to spend the extra time I had. I picked places including the Getty Museum, Kaiser Permanente Hospital, and a fabulous elementary school kindergarten class where I started something called *Pink Grandma's Drama Class.*

The first place I volunteered at was the world famous Getty Museum in Los Angeles. That was an experience in itself. The training was six weeks, every Saturday, from 9am to 3pm. Once finished, I knew everything there was to know about the Getty. I could now help out in any of the areas where they needed volunteers, including the information desk, the garden gate entrance, the Getty Theatre, and the Children's Exhibit.

My time at the Getty involved every other Sunday from 9 to 1. Not only did I enjoy my various volunteer positions, I gained a new respect and appreciation for art and the beautiful artifacts and statues I was exposed to. I would greet people by saying, "Good morning. I'm the Pink Lady of the Getty, and I'm here to answer your questions," which was fun! Quite often, visitors were from out of town and didn't speak English. But I found that a smile and a positive attitude can usually overcome any barrier, even language.

One day, I greeted a young couple with a darling little five-year-old girl. As they entered the museum, you could see the look of wonder in the little girl's eyes as she gazed at the many classic paintings on the wall. A few hours later, as the family was about to leave, the little girl, who now had a puzzled look on her face, asked, "If you're the Pink Lady of the Getty, where is your picture?" I just laughed and said, "They haven't hung it up yet."

One of my daughters, Harumi, teaches kindergarten. Being a grandmother and loving children, I thought of an idea after she mentioned that some of her students didn't have grandmothers, and wouldn't it be nice if they had a *Pink Grandma* to play with once a week.

Reading and acting out stories for kindergarteners was a natural for me. Talk about fun! That was the beginning of *Pink Grandma's Drama Class.*

There were 23 children in the class. As I was reading a story one afternoon, five-year-old Joey raised his hand. "Pink Grandma?" he asked. "Do you wear pink underwear?" I laughed and answered, "As a matter of fact I do." His response was funny. With a cute smile he continued, "I can't wait to tell my daddy." My daughter and I laughed and wondered what kind of response Joey might get from his dad. It was definitely a sign of the times we live in.

Pink Grandma's Drama Class

There are countless places where you can spend your valuable time as a volunteer and have some fun while simultaneously experiencing something valuable:

> *1. Volunteer as a law school witness where you actually get to act as a witness in mock trials and be immersed in the drama of a courtroom. At the UCLA School of Law, I played Ms. Palmer in Palmer v. Dunbar and then Ms. Dunbar in Dunbar v. Palmer! The judge would repeatedly have to remind me to stick to simple yes or no answers whenever I would begin to improvise on various stories. The jury thought that was funny.*
> *2. Volunteer to greet people arriving at the airport and help them find their airline, gate, or baggage-claim*

carousel. When I volunteered at the Burbank airport, I offered to be there at 5:45 in the morning, thinking it would be quieter. Boy was I wrong! 6 to 9am is the busiest time at an airport. Needless to say, time "flew by" whenever I was there.

3. Volunteer at your local police department. You can answer phones and field questions at the front desk. If you love helping people when they're in trouble, this might be the job for you.

4. Here's an interesting one... you can volunteer to be a mystery shopper. I tried it and had a great time. My first assignment was go to a grocery store and shop for certain items that had been advertised in the paper and then compare their prices to those of a competitor. I'm not very good with math, so I didn't last too long. But if you enjoy shopping and math, then mystery shopping may be just the thing for you.

5. One of the most rewarding experiences I ever had was volunteering at a local hospital. I had two jobs. The first was working in the gift shop and greeting the visitors. The second was interacting with the patients in their rooms. I would go around to all the rooms delivering newspapers and magazines. It was fun talking with the patients and being able to lift their spirits and make them smile. There was many a day when my spirits were lifted as well.

6. Working with veterans has proven to be a truly worthwhile experience at places like the VA Medical Center, retirement homes, and the local USO. Our veterans and active duty military who serve our country will truly appreciate your time and compassion.

There are literally hundreds of other places where you can volunteer your time. And when you do, you're actually helping yourself when you choose to help others. Some of the people you meet will become your friends. And there's always the chance that, if you're single, you just might find your new significant other.

So remember, people will forget what you said in your life, and people will forget what you did in your life, but people will never, ever forget how you made them feel with your positive attitude and the love and time you generously gave them.

PLACES TO VOLUNTEER

Adult Centers
Airports
American Cancer Society
American Red Cross
Animal Shelters
Consumer Affairs
Family Service Agencies
Farmer's Markets
Habitat for Humanity
Hospitals
Mentor Programs
Museums
Mystery Shoppers
Neighborhood Councils
Network for Good
Office Support

The Peace Corps
The Police Department
Public Libraries
Reading Programs (for Children or the Blind)
Salvation Army
Schools
Senior Corps
Sewing Groups
Theater Ushers
Thrift Shops
Tournament of Roses
University Mock Trials
Veterans & Active Duty
Wheels for Humanity
Zoo

Thoughts to Live By

A successful life can be measured by how one lives and loves in the time they're given. Don't ever complain about growing older, because there are so many people who are denied that privilege. Every one of us has what I call "human emotions." All of us want to be understood, forgiven, accepted, and loved. We're all the same in so many ways, yet we're also very different. That's what makes us unique and original.

I love to say "It ain't over till I say it's over." We should all be able to look forward to a full life and enjoy the challenge of reinventing ourselves. The secret is to make sure that our energy and zest for life continues. With the right attitude, it's never too late to discover the wealth and beauty that life can offer us. "To everything there is a season, and a time for every purpose under Heaven." So, let's grow older, not old; for I believe with all my heart and soul that the best is yet to come. To quote the following people:

Betty Friedan: "Age is not lost on youth, but it's just a new stage of opportunity and strength."

Garson Kanin: "Youth is the gift of nature, but age is a work of art."

Judge Judy: "When you get older, hopefully you have developed the smarts to know that if you wake up in the morning and you are vertical and your kids are healthy and out of the house, that's 90% of what it means to be happy."

There are many reasons that we have to love being 60 years young and over. I think the first is that you know who your friends are. They're the ones who don't desert you, be they new or old, who laugh and cry with you, and share the good times as well as the bad. As we get older, we tend to tighten our circle of friends and spend more time with those who share our interests and goals.

Someone once asked me about the pros and cons of aging. I thought about it for a while, and then I began to laugh until the tears rolled down my face, for there's no such topic as the pros and cons of aging. There are only the pros of aging. There are no cons, because if we didn't age, we wouldn't be here! I'm here to grow older – **not** old! I don't like the alternative, and I don't think you do either.

I think the question should be how one can age in the best way possible. Yes, we're aging, our bodies are slowing down and the eyes are not what they used to be. If you're female, our boobs, unless you had a boob job, are no longer perky. But we're still here. The aging process is improving every year. Years ago, life expectancy was 55. Then it became 60, then 70. Now we're living, working, and enjoying our lives into our 80s, 90s, and 100s. There are so many people at these ages who are "still" going strong. Remember, the shell does grow older and more brittle, but the mind and spirit can stay young if we nurture them the right way. A positive outlook truly does affect the aging process.

I like this anecdote about Janet and Paul who have been married for 49 years...

Janet made an appointment to see the doctor for her annual physical. When she came home she was very excited. "The doctor said that I have to have sex at least eight times a month," she told her husband. Paul smiled and said, "Put me down for two of those!"

We should choose to do things that do not give us stress or anxiety, but lots of pleasure. I call this stage "The Age of Being Appropriate." It's all about the passion. We have to take more steps than our parents and grandparents did to ensure that the rest of our lives will be meaningful and enjoyable. Now is your time for emotional clarity and enriching desires.

Be who you are. Don't obsess over your flaws – we all have them. Someone asked me what they should do about their wrinkles, and I said two things: If you can afford it, Botox them away. If you can't, learn to love the lines, for they are proof that you have lived a full and rich life. Another person asked me what I do to stay looking so young. And I replied, "Everything I can!"

Don't limit yourself. We all have the power to open ourselves up to change. USE IT! Think of yourself as a magnet for all the good things: meeting new people, enjoying new relationships, and traveling new roads to adventures you'd only dreamed were possible.

Ask yourself, "What do I want to do with the rest of my life?" Why not think big? Don't limit yourself.

Say, "I am capable, and I am unique." Say that everyday and it will empower you. There is a power to be reckoned with in each of us. When you think positively, you will see this power come into play in your mind, body, and spirit. It will take over to make you a better and happier person.

As I've said many times, the best way to predict the future is to create it. Don't just survive it. From this moment on, make sure you have a positive attitude in everything you set out to do. DO IT NOW AND DO IT FOR YOURSELF. Make yourself proud, and give yourself the opportunity to live your best life now. It is the only life you will ever have.

Aging is definitely a gift. For the first time in my life, I am finally the person I've always wanted to be. I am my own best friend. My contemporaries and I intend to enjoy being who we are today, for we know that we're not going to be around forever. While we're here, we're not going to waste time lamenting about what could have been, but will continue to look forward to what will be.

1. Your life is a drawing without an eraser.
2. What happens, happens for a reason. Deal with it.
3. Learn to have faith in something bigger than yourself.
4. Plan for tomorrow, but live for today.
5. Be eccentric now. Why wait until you're too old to be outrageous?

Exercises to Help Achieve Your Goals

The following questions will help guide you toward understanding how you can *Get Out* and get on with your life:

1. Are you willing to change your attitude, lifestyle, and old ideas?
2. Are you willing to invest in yourself and allow enough time to make this change successful?
3. Are you willing to be honest with yourself and take chances?
4. Are you willing to move past a problem and be open to a new solution?
5. Are you willing to put your whole heart and soul into the goal of finding a new life?

The best way to start out on a new path is to think about what you really want to do with the rest of your life. Now is the time to have emotional clarity, enriching desires, and exciting adventures. We are all different, and we will all age in different ways. Some say that old age, like retirement, is a time for people to slow down and get a few more cats. That's ridiculous. I'm not slowing down for anyone, and I don't need to march in anyone else's parade – but *my own.*

There are two things you must do to keep a good outlook and be able to reach your goals: Appreciate the age you are now, and enjoy this time of your life, because it is *all about you.* Today's world is letting us adapt ourselves to the art of aging, to value it, and to honor what it means to grow older in an era of unprecedented longevity, for we are embracing every stage of life as "Prime Time."

We can expect to lose some memory, but that's okay. And we can laugh at the things that happen when we do. For example, my car keys and my cell phone are always getting misplaced, but eventually I find them. And when I walk from one room to the next and suddenly ask, "Why did I come in here?" "What am I looking for?" I have to laugh at myself. So when you forget where you put your house keys and then find them in the front door, just smile and say, "It could be worse." It's better to be misplacing things and still be around to do it.

Sometimes, I will go to the market or to a party and someone will say, "Hey, Pink Lady, how are you?" And I cannot for the life of me remember their name. So what do I do? I smile and say, "You look wonderful. It's so good to see you." And then I walk away before I get into trouble. Such an attitude gives me the confidence I need to handle any situation in my own way and in my own time.

One Step at a Time

I believe there is life after 60. And those who are there should realize that the best is yet to come. You just have to find it, grab hold of it, and go for the gold with courage and conviction. Trust me when I tell you, it's the ride that makes the destination worth arriving at. Being free to be yourself is one of the joys that allows you to reach that fabulous, mysterious, exciting age of 60-plus. It's my time – it's your time. I say, "Go for it!" What do you have to lose? Use this valuable time to help yourself *Get Out.*

Taking one step at a time is something we should all do. Why don't we do it? Some of us are drowning in a sea of good intentions. We say, "I really have to first change the relationship I'm in," or "I have to first break this terrible habit," or "I will start my diet tomorrow."

Don't substitute talk for action. People spend time creating strategies to do things to help their situations, but they never carry them through. DON'T PROCRASTINATE. DO IT NOW! Not tomorrow, not next week, but NOW!

I was always on a diet, like most of us. I'd lose 5-7 pounds and, yes, gain it back in a little while. So I decided not to diet anymore – but instead make it a way of life by eating the right foods. So now when someone asks me how I keep in shape, I tell them "I don't diet anymore – my new and better eating habits are now my way of life."

Instead of thinking, "Should I start going out with a new man?" "Should I move out of my house into a retirement community?" "Should I clean the garage?" "Should I rearrange my closet?" start writing down the things you want to accomplish. At the end of the day, look at the paper and ask yourself, "Did I start toward the goals that I wanted to achieve?" If not, why not? Learn that nothing is impossible if you face the situation head-on and act on it. Make sure that when you say you want to change, you truly want to begin something new. Remember to start small, taking baby steps that continue to get bigger and wider as you reach your goal.

President Franklin Delano Roosevelt stated, "The only thing to fear is fear itself." I agree. Just do it! Don't worry about how long it will take. And don't worry about what anyone else might say. Just focus on how you will become more successful in your life. The more you do to change your lifestyle, the more confident and sure you will become.

Resolutions – Making It All Happen

Begin a program to change the things that are making you unhappy, uncomfortable, and unhealthy.

1. Create a simple plan. Take the first step slow and easy. You will see yourself generating more enthusiasm and confidence with time.
2. Get organized. Clean out one drawer, one closet, one cabinet, or one man at a time.
3. Let go of things that drain your energy. If there's a person, place, or thing that is sapping your strength, let it go! Your health and peace of mind are more important.
4. Take responsibility to help others. Use your special uniqueness and past experiences to show people what they are able to achieve. Giving of yourself will make you feel stronger and wiser. Whatever you can do to change and help someone else will also help you.

5. Rome wasn't built in a day. Be grateful for just being here now and able to grow older with a healthier mind, body, and spirit. Think of all the good times you're having and will continue to have with your family, friends, and significant others.

Secrets for Staying Young

What's the secret to truly being happy and keeping a youthful attitude? Well frankly, it's different for each of us. I'll tell you what my secret is... It's believing that I can and will succeed in whatever I set out to do. I think that I should love and believe in myself. I will use my body, my soul, and my life experiences to get the most out of these beautiful and exciting years of my life. The purpose of life, after all, is to live it – to taste each experience and make it your own.

Now is the time to decide whether to stay where you are or turn a new page. You deserve to have this part of your life be a beautiful and fantastic experience, full of passion and excitement. I never imagined I could have the fabulous relationships I have had after the loss of my husband. The key ingredient was opening myself up and being willing to take the chance to find that special person who would help me live again in an intimate and loving way.

Being aware of where you are at this point in your life is very important to your well-being. By taking one breath at a time, one moment at a time, you will be freer to see, hear, and do the things that make you feel good and to know just how special life can really be.

Who's to say what any of us can or cannot accomplish? Who's to say that life has to slow down and pass us by? Let's be positive and concentrate on living, loving, and laughing our way through the wonderful years we still have ahead of us. We are fortunate, by this time, to have increased our wisdom, creativity, and enthusiasm. We've been there, done that, and should be proud that we're *still* a force to be reckoned with.

But when we reinvent ourselves or reshape our way of life, there are a few things we should know. The most important is that we do not need anyone else's permission, as long as we're doing what's right for us. Equally important is to be open to all possibilities. The following suggestions will help:

1. Keep learning. Never let the brain become idle.
2. Take charge of your health. Preserve it if it's good, and improve it if it's not.
3. Tears will happen, but when they stop, move on.
4. Learn to count the wonderful and exciting experiences that made you the unique person you are.
5. Never stop challenging yourself. This is the time to continue to push yourself to create a new and positive way of life. The opportunities are there for you to seize the day and to live it your way.

You are no longer just a person with a past, but one who is living in the present and looking forward to reaching new goals in the future. There is no patent on reinvention, but an equal opportunity for everyone to find happiness. Don't be afraid to reinvent yourself by making this and every day the best it can possibly be, and by showing the world that age really is only a number.

Tips to Increase Your Willpower

In order to *Get Up, Get Out,* and move toward *Getting a Life,* we need to make sure we have the willpower to begin. Each time you say no to an old habit or practice a healthy new one, you're increasing your willpower and gradually getting stronger. Here are a few tips to help:

1. START SMALL ~ Do things you know you can accomplish to gain a sense of satisfaction by succeeding little by little.

2. EXERCISE YOUR WILL ~ Start your day by devoting time to a task you dislike, and then move on to the ones you really enjoy.

3. THINK HEALTHY ~ Eat nutritiously and get enough sleep so you can face the next day with increased energy and a healthier mind and body.

4. NEVER GIVE UP ~ Even when faced with disappointment, focus on the positive aspects of what you are accomplishing and be aware that, with your renewed willpower, you will have peace of mind.

5. REWARD YOURSELF ~ When you've demonstrated your ability to follow the steps above, celebrate by giving yourself a treat. You deserve it!

Mind Over Matter

Take the attitude that "it *will* all be okay." Have faith in yourself. Give yourself permission to enjoy life and to fall in love with the person you are. Yes, take time to smell the roses. I believe we *do* get better with age if we realize how lucky we are to be here. A positive attitude lets us feel good about who we are.

I'm here for the long run, and so are you. Bottom line: It's mind over matter – it's all in how you perceive the situation in which you find yourself. Choosing an upbeat outlook is a philosophy that we all can embrace. Here are five things you should repeat to yourself every day to help you get started on the road to *Getting Out:*

1. I will think of myself as successful.

2. I will have positive expectations in everything I do.

3. I will not dwell on my failures, nor will I repeat them.

4. I will surround myself with positive people and positive attitudes.

5. I will keep trying until I achieve the results I want.

We can call ourselves by any name we want, including "seasoned adults," "mature adults," or "prime-timers." Whatever name we use, we want to be sure that our life is still going forward in a productive and meaningful way. It's making sure that the adventure we started many years ago will keep moving forward and continue to open up new roads for us to travel. *THAT IS MIND OVER MATTER!*

So I ask you, are you ready to *Get Out* there and make today the first day of the "best" of your life? You can do this by learning to live longer, better, and wiser with a more positive state of mind. No matter how many birthdays go by, the lesson remains the same: Life is too short to spend valuable time doing things we do not enjoy or love to do. Let's not waste these precious years that we have left on things that don't make us feel good about ourselves or about the life we are living.

Someone once said, "Life is a succession of many moments, and to live each one individually is to be successful." You are now ready to *Get Up and Get Out!*

MISSION ACCOMPLISHED!

Section Three
GET IT ON!
Senior Sexuality and Relationships

*Love doesn't make the world go 'round. Love is what
makes the ride worthwhile.*

~ *Franklin P. Jones*

"To age or not to age," is not a question, but a
way of life. It is a fantastic, positive and passionate
feeling of understanding who we are, and where we're
going. Life itself is a joy, and definitely the *ride of a
lifetime.*

Relationships should be based on finding not
only a perfect mate within reason, but a lasting
friendship as well. We are all sexual by nature. How we
handle our sexuality is the difference between being
truly sexy and just being adorable. It feels good. It feels
right to have a relationship with someone you really
want to be with; for no matter what age we are, we all
need love and companionship in our lives.

111

Time changes so many things, including our physical, mental and emotional selves. As we age, our families, friends and significant others take on different roles in our lives. The basic core of loving someone keeps us grounded. Love is a strong, powerful and glorious experience. We will all go through many loves of different intensities throughout our journey. The one thing we must remember to do, is have the courage, passion and determination to find love and enjoy it, no matter what our age. No one really wants to be alone. Almost all of us crave some kind of intimacy, comfort and caring with someone who feels the same way about us.

Take it from me, sex DOES get better with age. Mae West once said, "Too much of a good thing can be wonderful at any age." I tell you in all honesty, with the help of our friends Viagra, estrogen cream and Astroglide, we can still be as bad or good as we want. Because at this time in our lives, with the right attitude, sex and intimacy can be as good as it gets.

When the spirit is willing but the body isn't, we must learn to improvise. We should have the self confidence to say what we want, and be comfortable enough in our relationships to swap calisthenics for intimacy. This makes us and our partner feel satisfied and loved. More tenderness and less testosterone can be very sexy in and of itself.

Remember that song in *A Chorus Line* that says, "I can't regret what I did for love?" Well, it's true. Whatever choices we've made, even the ones we called mistakes, can always be learned from. With all of these learning experiences, we can go to the next level by concentrating on positive choices with love and confidence. Hopefully, we'll be wiser and more understanding of our partner, and just as important, ourselves. Love is for all of us! And intimacy in all forms makes relationships warm and tender.

A few months ago, I heard a famous actress, 75 years young, say: "Aging reminds me of different countries in our world...

From 18 to 22 is like Africa – Half driven and half wild.
From 23 to 33 is like Canada – Well developed and open to trade.
From 34 to 44 is like India – Very hot and quite relaxed.
From 45 to 50 is like France – Getting cozy and warm.
From 51 to 59 is like Britain – Staid and elegant.
From 60 to 65 is like Yugoslavia – Lost the war but learned from past mistakes.
From 66 to70 is like Russia – Very wide borders which are unpatrolled and take courage to leap over.
From 70 and on is like Tibet – Wise beyond age, strong-willed, and ready to visit all the other countries."

"Can We Talk?"

Hopefully, we can talk about everything and anything that has to do with today's mature-adult sexuality and lovemaking. I hate to burst the public's bubble about those over the age of 60 and even into the 90's, but seniors are rapidly becoming the biggest online dating-service users in the country. Watch out, you 30, 40, and 50-year-olds! Our over 60 crowd is on the move, having the best times of our lives in our bedrooms and everywhere else!

Where do I begin? Let's start with me. I am 84 years young and continue to feel sexy, sensual and desirable. I believe it's our attitude about ourselves which leads us to being able to have a fulfilling relationship with a significant other. I definitely feel romantic and, yes, thank you God, continue to enjoy the

My Guy

beauty of intimacy. I mean, c'mon.... I'M NOT DEAD! Age has nothing to do with having a fantastic, wondrous, romantic love life. I enjoy being a sexy, sizzling, scintillating senior!

The word intimacy has many meanings. A lot of people think it refers to just sex, but that's not true. Sex to me, means an exercise – a physical means of expression between two people. Intimacy has a warmer and more meaningful definition – It's the art of two people touching, holding, caressing, kissing and being aware of each other's physical and mental needs. Don't laugh, intimacy can also happen over a meal or a cup of coffee. Just looking into someone's eyes and smiling can give us a warm, cozy, comfortable sensation and often a physical response for a man (and for a woman, too).

Today's single older adult should no longer be stereotyped. Being at this time in our life comes with its own challenges – economically, socially, physically, mentally, and spiritually. But it also offers us new and exciting opportunities to grow, to learn, and to experience new romantic adventures. We now have a chance to do all the things we've always wanted to do, but never could until now. WHY? Because for most of us, raising a family and working have interfered with the amount of time allowed for intimacy with our partners. It is NOW our time to enjoy it all without those barriers.

We have to ask ourselves truthfully, what do I really need right now? What do I want at this point? What kind of relationship am I looking for? I know exactly what I wanted in the beginning – I wanted to have fun, a bit of romance and companionship, but most of all, friendship. I wasn't looking for love right away, if at all. The feeling of someone wanting me for who I am was more important to me. I wanted a man who I could talk to, laugh with, hold hands with and kiss comfortably.

To achieve a great romantic relationship, one must have the mindset to want to be close to another person and to enjoy them in every way. In order to become more aware of each other's needs and wants, intimacy can also come from talking about family, past experiences and things that interest both of you. To be able to *talk and laugh* with someone during our most intimate moments is something rare but achievable with the right partner and the right frame of mind.

Age does not negate sexuality – if anything, it enhances it. We have definitely reached a point where we should realize that it's our right, at this wonderful and fabulous time, to be considered sexy, vibrant, and fun-loving. There's nothing wrong with learning new things at this age to enhance intimacy. We should never be afraid of trying something new, because often times, it can ultimately become exciting and satisfying. And we must never, ever buy into the "too old for sex" stereotype...

I'd like to tell you about five men whom I see every day. I know that some of you probably see these same gentlemen in your lives. As soon as I wake up, WILL POWER helps me get out of bed. Then I go to see

JOHN. After that, CHARLIE HORSE comes along, and when he's here, he takes up a lot of my time and attention until I give him a workout.

When CHARLIE leaves, ARTHUR RITIS shows up and stays the rest of the day (he doesn't like to stay in one place very long, so he takes me from joint to joint). After such a busy day, I'm really tired and truly happy to get into bed with BEN GAY. WHAT A LIFE!

All joking aside, being sexual today is not only possible, it's ours for the taking. It is now the norm for what's happening within our generation. Intimacy makes us feel vibrant and alive! Isn't that what we're all looking for? I do know that most of us want companionship and "someone who has our back." AND, it's also very comforting when someone has your front as well.

Today, when you meet someone and they look interesting, there's nothing wrong with asking them to have a cup of coffee. We've been through the "age of innocence." We've been through the "sexual revolution." Most of us have been married once, twice, or more, and many of us have had more than one affair. Social etiquette has changed in the last 50 years. We need to change with the times as well.

We need to start each new relationship with the thought, "I have found a new friend." It doesn't matter their age, or whether they're younger or older than you. As long as you have a good time, who cares? Start from what I call the "instant likeability test." Is there chemistry? Is there a spark? If there is, go for it! Do not be afraid of rejection. What's the worst that can happen? If you're not totally vulnerable, you cannot totally love or be loved.

Look, NOW IS OUR TIME! It all depends on your attitude. If you give yourself permission, you'll open up the chance of finding that someone you want to spend the rest of your life with.

What does it take to have a meaningful intimate relationship? The number one thing is for both people to come into the partnership with the right attitude. It takes courage and honesty to make it work. It also takes what I call "an open door policy" of absolute consideration for the other person's feelings and needs.

As a mature adult, you don't have to answer to anyone about the decisions you're making in your love life. Those decisions are yours and yours alone. Do what truly makes *you* happy. Follow your own inner desires. No matter what age we are, it doesn't stop us from wanting to *be pleased* and to *please* the one we truly care about.

It's perfectly okay for us to do whatever it takes to keep those juices flowing in our minds and bodies. Ladies, don't stop buying that sexy lingerie or stop wearing that perfume that arouses him. Continue to flirt and tease and have a good time. Why not? Gentlemen, the same goes for you. There's nothing sexier than a man in nice clothes wearing super-sexy cologne with a rose in one hand and a box of her favorite candy in the other. *And that ring for her finger won't hurt either!*

WHY NOT STAY ALIVE?
       WHY NOT STAY VIBRANT?
              WHY NOT STAY EXCITING?

I believe there's someone out there for each and every one of us. Remember that song *For Every Man There's a Woman?* You will meet the person you were meant to meet at this stage of your life if you're willing and persistent enough to let yourself be open to new adventures and to explore new and exciting ways to please each other – in *and* out of bed.

> *Do whatever it takes to get and keep that special person you want by your side.*

As one who's been there and done that, and is definitely still doing it, I realize it's not easy to look for a new romance after one is widowed, divorced or has lost a partner. But life does go on! We are all human in our need to be loved and pampered by someone who makes us feel alive and well in every way. So make sure you choose someone who makes you feel good about yourself and with whom you want to share your most intimate and pleasurable moments.

I've always believed that we give off vibrations to other people, both positive and/or negative. Those positive wave lengths which are full of energy and excitement will have a lot to do with meeting Mr. or Ms. Right.

What exactly do we mean by the word "sexuality"? I think it's about having fun with who we are and who we're with. Remember, as funny as it sounds, having a sexual encounter helps our health by relaxing us and providing a source of exercise and calorie burning, plus a good night's sleep. It's not just about having intercourse. It's not just an exercise – up, down... in, out... on, off. Oh no, it's much, much more. It's definitely what makes the Earth move and the sky blue. If you don't hear yourself exclaiming "OH MY GOD" at least 11 times in your most intimate moments, *"you may not be doing it right!"*

> *When I'm good,*
> *I'm VERY good!*
> *But when I'm bad,*
> *I'm EVEN BETTER!*
> ~ Mae West

It's a fact that we laugh more and we take better care of ourselves when we're in a relationship. It's a win-win situation. Sex is not just about going to bed with someone, for one can be sexual out of bed as well. I know what you're thinking: "When one reaches 60, 70, 80 and up, things don't happen like they did at 30, 40 and 50." Well, true! We know about the loss of estrogen in women as they age, and we know about the loss of testosterone in men. BUT REAL SEX IS MORE THAN THAT, THANK GOODNESS!

Senior sexuality is a beautiful, warm, loving way to enjoy this time of our lives. It is truly a wonderful feeling to be able to respect and trust another person once again. Forget about your chronological age.

Instead, think about how young you feel. *Get Up* and begin your search for your new soul mate. *Get Out* your best attitude, put a smile on your face, get dressed in your nicest outfit, and begin to *Get a Life*. You will never regret the joy you will find in sharing your life once again with someone who truly cares who you are.

It's possible at any age to find deep love – a soul mate – long after you thought it was impossible. Is it luck, karma or accidental that love can happen to us later in our lives? Many people I talk to say the same things: "I thought I was too old to find another love." "I thought because I am this age that no one would find me attractive anymore." "I thought I could never be intimate with anyone other than my husband/wife or significant other." Life changes, circumstances give us the opportunity to revive our sexuality all over again. And, many times, we find that we can enjoy intimate, romantic relations more now than ever before.

The real key to keeping things alive and enjoyable in the most important room in the house, the bedroom, is having an open line of communication with our other half. Without communication, the best love affair is over before it has a chance to begin. My mother once told me that if I can't talk to my partner the next morning, then what we did the night before means nothing. It was definitely good advice.

Remember to leave yourself open to learn about a person; for there are those who have been married numerous times or have experienced many affairs who feel they've never found their true soul mate even after years of living together. Think of it as an adventure; a mystery to be solved; a book to open and enjoy to the very end.

There may come a time when we begin to find sex with our partners routine and unexciting. The problem could be on either side. Here's where communication comes in. We should never be too busy to talk about it. Just turning over and saying, "it's okay, see you in the morning" doesn't do it. This is where problems begin in a relationship. I realize we all have busy schedules, but we must take the time to talk with our partner to resolve these intimate-moment challenges. If left alone, the distance will grow between you. Honesty in the moment opens up the line of communication and can lead to a solution.

If you see a decline in your romantic time together, solve the problem now. It's okay to talk about it, but it's more important to do something about it. Remember, it's always fun to try new things. Sex can get very old, and I'm not talking about chronological age. You can get bored with each other without even realizing it. You need to have some "newness" to elevate your desires – to bring back the joy of intimacy which *does not die* at a certain age.

There are quite a few ways to help our intimate moments get better. As we get older, we become more knowledgeable in some of these ways, by reading and watching programs about sex. A lot of us are viewing adult entertainment to enhance our love lives. There are some good 'tools' out there to make our bedroom activities more interesting. Sex shops are not just for the young. A trip to one to find these gadgets can be fun, and also a way of bringing two people closer together; the couple who shop together, play together.

Keeping an open mind about sex and intimacy can make us feel liberated in what we do at this wonderful and creative stage of our lives. It's our prerogative to decide whether we will just date, live together, or marry. Whatever makes us happy is what's right for us. One of my friends, for example, got married at 79. When someone asked her about sex, she responded, "We have a wonderful sex life. There are some physical challenges, but you just have to be patient and learn to be creative." God bless them!

Each and every moment at this time is very precious to all of us. We have learned throughout our lives, that when we find happiness with another individual, we must not be selfish. We have to create a unified, loving place for both of us to be in. And if one gives a little more than the other at different times, so what? If two people can be together and spend time loving, laughing, and living, that's what makes an exciting and joyous life continue to be worthwhile.

SO, CAN WE TALK? YOU BET WE CAN! WE CAN TALK ABOUT SENIOR SEXUALITY AND BE PROUD TO BE ALIVE, AND CONTINUE TO SHARE OUR LIVES WITH OUR PRESENT PARTNER OR OUR NEW-FOUND SOUL MATE.

I'm now ready to tell you where and how to meet, keep, and enjoy that special new romantic person in your life. I'M READY AND I HOPE YOU ARE!

What's "It" All About?

Let me begin by saying, WELCOME TO SENIOR SEX CITY, USA! with its population of lusty, sexy, available, mature adults who just happen to be in their senior years.

How many of us have dreamed of a knight in shining armor or a sexy supermodel coming into our lives and sweeping us off our feet? Come on everyone, admit it. We've all had this fantasy – this vision of what "love eternal" could be.

Oh, those three words... ROMANCE, LOVE and SEX! Wow, I get goose bumps when I think about how they make me feel. I know you also must feel a certain rush when you think of being intimate with the love of your life.

First, I want to make myself quite clear: This subject is a very touchy one, and it may make some of you feel a bit uncomfortable. But in today's world, you have to get used to the language before you can truly enjoy a fun, romantic, intimate sexual encounter which will lead to a beautiful relationship. I realize that sex, intimacy, sexuality, and all those words are still private to some of us. But today, it's a different world. I believe we must "USE IT OR LOSE IT." We must be ready and able to discuss all of these personal matters as a new relationship develops or as we continue in our current one.

Wow, where do we start? Is there anyone in this world who *doesn't* want to be sexy or sensual? Or even sizzling? I think, DOWN DEEP, every one of us does. We've always wanted to be able to attract the opposite sex, or for some, the same sex. No matter, we all want that other half of the equation in our lives and in our beds.

Someone asked me why I think sex is so important at this stage in my life. I said, "I believe that sex reaffirms who we are. It gives us a bond with that other person with whom we're spending our time. It gives us a beautiful sense of truly being alive and awakens our feelings that life can still be exciting."

We joke about sex and what it can or cannot do for us:

A friend of mine couldn't get her significant other of thirty-five years to go to a party she wanted to attend. He kept saying he didn't really feel like it, didn't really like the people. Out of the blue, she offered, "If you go to this party tonight, when we get home, I'll give you the best sex you've ever had." Guess what happened! In the morning, he laughingly admitted, "I would've gone anyway because I love you, but what you said excited me and made me feel young and vital again, and I wanted to be with you even more." YES!!! There are many ways to re-awaken our sexual drives.

When older people are asked about sex, many say it gets better as we age. Why do you suppose that is? I think it's because we're more relaxed and can enjoy the moment without thinking about how busy we are, that the kids might walk in, or "Oh dear, I might get pregnant!"

I tell people these are truly our most sensual years. It's when our energy level equals our adventurous curiosity to discover new ways to satisfy ourselves in the relationships we're cultivating. And, we realize that this is our last hurrah, so why not live every moment and enjoy the freedom that comes with aging.

Love Is In the Air

I'd like to start with the word LOVE. The dictionary offers three definitions:

1. An affectionate concern for another person.
2. An intense sexual desire for someone.
3. To become enamored or sexually attracted to someone.

Whether you're 55, 65, 75, 85 or over, it's never too late to fall madly in love. Our minds, our bodies, our spirits are still capable of feeling that little *ping*, or whatever you want to call it, when we meet that person who can make us feel a little breathless when we're with them. That biological chemistry that starts percolating in our bodies can be good to the very last drop.

Not long ago I read about a couple in their late 70s, who were married for over 40 years. They said that when they met, they became friends and then lovers. They said they remained in love throughout their marriage because they were friends first and bed partners second. They were lovers in every way, at all times – always kind, respectful and caring about their partner's wants and needs, and *in love* with who their partner was.

To be wanted, cherished, and admired – to have and care about someone else – should be a part of all our lives. It's a natural instinct. It's nothing to be ashamed of but rather something to be proud of. You are never, ever too old to have these emotional feelings and physical desires. Why doesn't the world understand that the emotions of love, excitement, passion, desire and caring never have to die. The intensity might change, but the feelings remain.

Never use the word *impossible*. I believe you should go at life with abandon. Give it all you've got and life will give it all back to you with passion and enthusiasm. It's been said that the secret of life isn't in what happens to us, but rather what we *do* with what happens to us.

Lovers of all ages want a physical and spiritual relationship, and it's within everyone's grasp to be able to connect with someone who feels the same way. But it does take a bit of work on both sides. It's not, and never will be, a one- way street. Even if the relationship is 60/40, it will still work if there's a strong foundation of love built upon a continued pursuit of romance, respect and pride in who you are with.

No one is counting how many times we think we've found Mr. or Ms. Right. But we do have an advantage. We're at a stage in life where we have the time to explore different people to find the one who's right for us. So please, don't get paranoid, don't freak out, and don't panic. Be who you are... that wonderful, energetic, kind, sensitive, caring person whom anyone would love to go out with and be with in a loving relationship. Keep your mind in that place, and IT WILL HAPPEN TO YOU! *Just leave yourself open to what the Universe has to offer – a world full of people like you who want to connect.*

I think that mature adults are better at handling the challenges of a new romance because at this stage, our horizons (life's timelines) are becoming shorter. We are now able to separate what is really important from what's not, because we see that time is precious and should not be wasted on people who aren't committed to having a true and meaningful relationship that brings joy to both parties. I have learned through the years that if it's not working to your standard or what makes you happy – LET IT GO.

ATTENTION, ACCEPTANCE, APPRECIATION and AFFECTION are the four A's that are important in building a bond of understanding with our future partners. And let's not forget the "chemistry" – that all-important feeling that makes two people want to connect from the very moment they meet. It doesn't matter how old or how young we are, we know when it's right.

I've talked about senior sexuality at this point because I feel it's a precursor to getting out there and beginning to date to find that special someone. I realize that for most of us it's a huge leap of faith to go from *Getting Up and Getting Out* to actually begin *Getting a Life!*

This leads me into one of the most important parts of my book: Dating. I know the world has a preconceived idea of when, where and at what age people might find new relationships. I'm here to tell you, through my own experiences, *there is no age limit* on dating and searching to find a new partner or companion. And in my case, as in some of yours, it might take a few "not really right for us" people, to find Mr. or Ms. Right. BUT THAT'S OK – just keep looking!

You've Come a Long Way, Baby!

That expression is really quite true. Today, it's okay to date people younger/older than you are. Why not? As long as you're emotionally and spiritually in tune with each other, the physical parts will come together. We all want the same things in a mate: someone with a sense of humor, who is dependable, considerate, definitely someone who respects who we are, and enjoys some of the same things we do. We must be open to learning and accepting the other person's ideas of what's important and enjoyable.

We have to keep in mind that priorities change at different stages in our lives. When we were young, it was that first impression that counted. By now we should have reached the age of wisdom to get beyond making that first impression so important. To a degree, age does change our appearance, but our spirit, mind, and heart are still there. And we each have something wonderful to give one another. We must allow others a chance to really show who and what they're really like.

Please don't think for one minute that because you reach 50, 60, 70, 80, and up that your sexual needs, desires and romantic feelings are no longer part of your life – even though it's a difficult subject for your families to think or hear about.

Here's what happened to me… I can remember the first time I had a date about a year after Walter passed away. I was a little apprehensive but filled with anticipation, because after 40 years, I had just begun to date again. So what does every red-blooded, mature adult in their 70s do? I called my kids to tell them what happened on my very first date. I was so excited and happy that it went so well. I started to tell my oldest son, Michael, when he suddenly stopped me and blurted out, "TMI!"

"What," I asked, "does that mean?"

"Too Much Information," he explained.

Hearing this, I knew what I had to do. Two weeks later, my son called me on a Sunday morning and wondered, "Mom, I called you last night at 11:30 and you didn't answer. Then I was concerned, so I called you again at 1:30 this morning and there was still no answer. Where were you?"

Smiling to myself I replied, "TMI!"

That was the last time my kids ever questioned me about my dating experiences.

And that's as it should be. At this age, we know what's appropriate and what our comfort zones are. We're perfectly capable of setting our own boundaries. The first thing we have to remember is to be honest with ourselves as well as with our families and friends when addressing the role sex plays in our lives.

Wise Words for Senior Dating

Dating as seniors is definitely a bit tougher than when we were dating in our middle years. But it is not impossible. I know in my heart that it is easier to date someone close to your own age for many reasons. Why? It makes it easier to communicate with each other on all levels because you're coming from a similar period in time and from some of the same experiences. But without a doubt, if two people are on the same wave length, no matter what the difference in their ages, it will work.

Don't get discouraged or disenchanted when you think all the good people are either taken or no longer around. Just because you haven't found that certain someone, doesn't mean you won't. No matter what your age is, you can begin right now – today – to find that special person. It just takes patience, commitment and a positive attitude to put yourself out there to be seen and heard by the right one.

Here are a few tips that will make it easier for you to do this:

1. After the loss of a significant other, give yourself time to heal and to adjust to your new life as a single person.
2. Start the dating process slow and easy, and try not to take rejection personally. If it doesn't work out, just move on.
3. If you go out with someone on a few dates and discover that you don't share at least a few of the same interests, it's OK. You should never give up hope. You will meet the right one when you least expect it.
4. Make a list of what you DO NOT WANT in a relationship. This will help clarify what you DO want. Look at your past relationships and see why they didn't work. What do you think caused the breakups? Writing it down will show you the recurring behavior of the type of person who made you TURN OFF, TUNE OUT, and TURN AWAY.
5. Now make a list of what you DO WANT in a relationship... like physical appearance, age range, interests, etc., so you don't waste time with someone who doesn't fit the profile that you prefer.

In the next two or three decades, medical and scientific advancement will extend our lives to an unprecedented length. It will be the norm to live and enjoy life well into our hundreds. So you'd better make sure you really like the person you choose as a mate/partner/significant other, because you could be together for another 30-35 years!

I believe there are certain elements that make up how we deal with our senior sexuality...

1. *Cause and effect: "What you sow, so shall you reap."*
2. *Belief and control: You must believe you're in charge of your own destiny and that there are no limits to what you can accomplish. Believing creates reality.*

Everything you need to make the rest of your life the best it can be is in you right now. All you have to do is find the right combination to unlock it. With senior sexuality, we must learn to get rid of any self-doubt and to trust our intuition and GO FOR THE GOLD.

Remember to LOVE AND LIVE FULL – AND DIE EMPTY. The journey from where we are to where we want to be is a glorious one, filled with love, pain, sorrow, joy, and adventure. It is definitely worth all the time it takes to get there.

Finding the Humor in Dating

Let's talk about getting out there and meeting people. In our mature years, we sometimes become complacent about ourselves when we're living alone. We might tend to let ourselves go. We gain a few pounds, let our hair get a little too gray, and lose track of what's happening in the world around us. It's never too late to change these habits. When we want to start looking for a new relationship, appearance and attitude are two very important matters that need to be addressed.

I was in a documentary film called *Beauty Culture*. It dealt with women of all ages, from little five-year-old beauty queens to famous models in their eighties. One of the scenes shows me with a professional makeup artist asking me, "Pink Lady, why do you put your makeup on at 6 in the morning?" The next scene has me all dressed up in a sequined outfit, makeup and hair done, sitting on a stool and saying to the camera, "The reason I put my makeup on at 6am is that I'm single. And if the doorbell rings and it's the FedEx man, I want to be ready for him!"

ANNENBERG SPACE
FOR PHOTOGRAPHY

BEAUTY
CULTURE

If you're looking for Mr. or Ms. Right, why not treat it like a game plan? Re-evaluate yourself first. Look for ways to accentuate your good points. Most important, circulate in groups where you would most likely meet a man or a woman whom you'd like to date. Good examples of where to go: Home Depot, Pep Boys, car clubs, sporting events, churches, temples, dance classes, fitness clubs, college extension classes, and all those volunteer places I listed.

And definitely, and I repeat, definitely, when you meet someone you think you might like to spend some time with, overcome any inhibitions you have and say, "Hi there. I'm so- and-so." Keep yourself open and available. You won't have any relationships if you don't put yourself out there. NO ONE WILL KNOCK ON YOUR DOOR IF THEY DON'T KNOW YOU'RE THERE.

There are certain things that one must be careful of in the dating game. Just ask me, I've been through a lot of them. You've gotta be aware when a red flag waves in your face. Don't be duped and fall for it:

1. Dating a person who says, "I'm single – my partner and I are separated." BS! They're married and they're NOT going anywhere! They're especially not going into a meaningful relationship with you!
2. When you go places with your date, like restaurants, movies, or sporting events, watch how they treat the service people around them. Are they demanding? Are they nasty and denigrating? Or are they kind and polite? Because how they are with others is a really good indication of how they'll be with you.

3. Do they constantly talk about their past wives/husbands or girlfriends/ boyfriends? Be careful. It's always good to know about someone's past life, but when they dwell on it, it's a red flag. It means they don't want to get on with their life. They're stuck in the past.

4. When you do share an intimate experience, and get out of bed, if you can't have a conversation afterward, you have no basis on which to continue the relationship. Sex is only one part of the equation. It's the exercise part; it's not the only part. You need to be able to communicate with the other person about all facets of your relationship.

5. The most important red flag to watch for is how the person treats you. Is it with respect? Is it with a caring attitude? Is this someone who's acting as if they want to be your soul mate? Is this someone who shows you that they are not only truly proud to be with you but want to be with YOU more than anyone else in the world?

It took me a year and a half after losing Walter to get the courage to begin to date. It wasn't easy, but if you really put yourself out there and say, *I'm okay. I'm ready to make new friends and start dating,* it will happen.

Believe me, it took a lot of soul-searching and talking to myself to find the courage, as a single woman after 39 years of marriage and someone in her 70's, to take the first step in finding a new partner. The time finally came when one of my dear friends talked me into going with her to a "bereavement singles" event. You won't believe what happened next.

I got all dressed up. I prepared my psyche for meeting new people, particularly men. When I walked into the bereavement class, a gentleman walked over to me and, with a big smile, took my hand and said something I was not prepared for: "Well, good evening, pretty lady. From one loser to another, welcome to Singles At Large." With those words, I turned around, walked out and went home.

Some people might do what I did. Others would have gone in and checked out the rest of the group. I chose not to. It might not have been the right thing to do, but for me at that time, it was.

I knew that I was not a "loser." I knew that I was not a "victim." I was a woman who had lost her husband, but I was definitely a person who was worthwhile, vital and alive. And I kept repeating to myself, as I cried driving home, "Jackie, it's okay. Life is full of experiences. Learn to take the good with the bad, and get on with your life." THERE IS A TOMORROW!

All of us have family who want to introduce us to people. I'm no different. One of my cousins called and told me about a doctor friend of hers who would be "perfect" for me. Beware the word perfect...

A few days later I got a call from the doctor, and we set up a blind date. He sounded very nice on the phone, except he seemed a little abrupt in his manner. I got a sense that he was used to giving orders to people. In spite of that, I accepted the invitation to dinner. It was a Friday evening, about 6, and I was ready and looking great, when I opened the door.

There stood Dr. Paul. Not bad looking, a little bald, about 5 ft. 9, dressed very sharp, and carrying a beautiful pink rose in his hand. I asked him in and offered him a glass of wine. He turned to me and said in a very authoritative voice, "I think we should go to bed first. Then we can have our drink and dinner and be more relaxed."

I looked at him, smiled, and said, "Take your rose, take your dinner and your drink, and..." (use your imagination here), as I led him to the door. I was not that needy or hungry!!!

I called my cousin and said, "I love you very much, but don't you ever, ever fix me up with someone like that again. I would much rather make myself a scrambled egg and watch a movie on TV than go out with somebody like that." And that's just what I did.

My next "adventure" in the world of dating was at Starbucks. I am a Starbucks aficionado – I'm there once or twice a day. When I was volunteering at the Getty every other Sunday, I would stop at Starbucks at 8 in the morning. I noticed, for a few Sundays, there was a very nice looking gentleman reading his paper and drinking a latte at a corner table. He would always smile at me and we would exchange a few words of greeting.

One Sunday, we actually started a conversation, and he asked me out to dinner for the following Saturday. His name was Larry. That Saturday evening, he picked me up and said he hoped I liked Italian restaurants, as he was taking me to his favorite one.

We drove for about 15 or 20 minutes talking and laughing. He seemed to be a very sweet and nice person. He pulled up to a home in a lovely area of Hollywood. I was a little surprised, and I asked him, "Where's the restaurant?" "Oh," he said, "right here," as he knocked on the door, and a woman wearing an apron answered.

It turned out to be a delightful and surprising evening. The lady who had opened the door was his daughter – a famous Los Angeles chef who catered dinners in her home to groups of 10 or more. That night, there were about 20 people sitting around intimate tables, enjoying the best Italian food I've ever had. Larry and I went out a few more times, but then we went our separate ways. There was nothing wrong with Larry; there was just no real chemistry between us. And at this stage of my life, I didn't want to waste time. Time is a very precious commodity to us now and should never be wasted on those who cannot give us what we want and need to be fulfilled and happy.

In dating, you run into lots of different situations. Some of them are good and some not so good. The main thing to remember is to keep going out and testing the waters.

The "dating game" is exactly what it proclaims. It's a game. It's going out with a person and seeing if there's a common connection that would make you want to go out with them again. In dating that person, it's all about getting to know them and seeing if there is any electricity for a lasting relationship. And, sometimes, you can make a true friend for life who doesn't always have to be a bed partner.

We have to remember not everyone has to be Mr. or Ms. Right. They can turn out to be just great friends.

Places to Meet That Someone Special

Where do I look for love and in what places can I find it? I know that many of you have asked the same questions and would like to find the answers, so let's get started.

A great way to begin meeting people, as I've mentioned, is to volunteer. Another fun way is by joining a group such as Toastmasters, neighborhood councils or chambers of commerce, religious organizations, etc. There are many groups and organizations that could use your help and where you will find people with similar interests. Here are some places where you might find the new love of your life:

> 1. Coffee bars, bookstores and libraries now have armchairs and comfortable couches where you can sit and read and say hello to the people next to you who share your interests. For instance, if you're at the bookstore and you're interested in sports, murder mysteries or outdoor activities, go to the appropriate section and you'll find others who like the same things. **Beware of people in the murder mystery section who linger too long.**

2. Join a group to see movies, theatrical productions, concerts, museums and art exhibits. Playing cards, going to dances and attending wine-tasting events can be fun, too. Volunteer to usher or work backstage with your local theatre group. Children's theater groups generally need a lot of help also. Wow, what a great way to meet other grandparents – many of whom are single!

3. Cruises. Because they're away from their daily routines, people on cruises are more open to meeting others and exploring new relationships. Check online or with your travel agent for cruises catering to mature single adults.

4. Take a bus trip. Even if you get on the bus alone, by the end of the day, you'll have met everyone on your tour. Try one-day excursions at first, then graduate to two- or three-day ones. You will meet people like yourself, who want adventure, fun and companionship.

5. There are many tours to casinos and resort areas that are not too far from your home. Become part of a travel group. Your senior center – pardon me, your adult center – will have tons of day trips that are inexpensive and full of exciting things to do.

6. Religion. Many of us belong to churches or synagogues, and most of them offer a variety of cultural activities. Depending on your particular interests, this is another way to get yourself involved with a whole new group of like-minded individuals.

7. Physical activities. (I don't mean jumping up and down on a bed. Well, not yet, anyway.) Horseback riding, bowling, walking, hiking, tennis, golf, skiing, swimming, and even mountain climbing (for those of us who can still climb) can bring you together with other singles. Another great gathering place for the single community is a fitness club. Besides trying to get trim and slim, these singles have already learned to *Get Up and Get Out*. Now they're well on their way to *Get a Life* and meet someone new.

When I first became a widow, I thought taking up a sport would give me a chance to make new acquaintances. So I started tennis lessons. After five lessons, my darling tennis instructor said, "Pink Lady, there are things that are for us and things that are not for us. I'd advise you to take up golf." I thought, "Okay, golf it is." I went out and bought a golf outfit, gave the tennis one away, and bought brand-new golf clubs. After all, I was going to be the new Brook Henderson!
I really did try. I looked really cute in my golf clothes, and I had spent a fortune on the golf clubs. But by the end of ten lessons, my illustrious, award-

winning instructor said, "Pink Lady, you have a lot of enthusiasm and tons of energy, but the worst golf swing I've seen in a long time!" Sooo... I gave away my lovely clothes and sold my golf clubs, and thus ended my attempts at meeting people in the sports arena.

8. High school and college adult education classes like Oasis and Encore programs. At these places, there are classes in everything from learning a new language to gourmet cooking. By the way, a cooking class is a fantastic way to meet a prospective date. You can always ask them to your house for dinner and prepare the new recipe you just learned in class.

9. Politics. Wow – this is a fun and stimulating way to meet like-minded people. Not only will you stay informed about what's happening in the world, but by volunteering at the local chapter of the party of your choice, you'll meet others with similar political interests.

10. Go clubbing. I don't mean bar-hopping or hitting people over the head. The clubs I'm talking about are country clubs, bridge clubs and garden clubs.

When you actually find someone you'd like to know better, the first plan should be to find a place where you can just talk. Sharing a breakfast, lunch, or a Starbucks moment is always a good place to begin. The next step is going to an event that interests both of you. Beginnings like this, slow and easy, help to build a solid relationship.

The common thread in these ideas of where to meet people is that you have to think outside of the box. I've met people at baseball games for my grandkids, at seminars at my brokerage firm, and at senior workshops. There are tons of places to meet people. Just think about it. If you don't get out there, you'll never find the person you were destined to meet. *So Get Up, Get Out, and Get on your way to a New Life.* The ideas I've presented here hopefully will open up ways for you to experience brand new adventures and form new relationships.

Don't ever give up on finding Mr. or Ms. Right – they're out there. You may have to go through one, two, or a dozen dates, but remember, keep your sense of balance and humor intact. Your energy, your personality, and your attitude will make the biggest difference in finding that significant other. Believe me, the feeling you'll get when you meet the right one will make all the effort you put into it worthwhile.

Now that we've discussed where you can find a date, I'm going to tell you where they're not. They are not in your kitchen, where you just grabbed some chocolate chip cookies and cold milk. They're not in your garden, where you're in your old Levi's and straw hat. They're not in your living room where you're in your robe, reading or watching television. They're not in your garage, where you're in your old t-shirt sorting tools.

But they're out there, in the world, and that's where you have to be in order to meet them. You've got to be alive, energetic, enthusiastic, and looking your very best, with a smile on your face and a spring in your step that communicates to everyone that you're available and ready to have a meaningful and fun relationship. AND that you are not old, simply aging in step. The rules of dating have changed. The conventions we lived by in our 30's, 40's and 50's might still apply, but they need to be updated.

Such was the case with my friend, Bessie, who is living in a retirement community and looking for male companionship. She went into the Activity Lounge where the men were playing poker. Smiling to herself, she raised her clenched fist in the air and announced in a loud voice: "Anyone who can guess what's in my hand can have his way with me tonight."

A gentleman in the rear of the room shouted out, "AN ELEPHANT." Without missing a beat, she lowered her arm, looked at her fist, turned it over, raised it in the air again and said, "CLOSE ENOUGH." Maybe we should all approach the subject like Bessie did.

Here are some guidelines that I think will help:

1. It is definitely okay for the woman or the man to make the first phone call after the initial meeting.

2. Stay in the moment. On the first date, why not just have a good time? Most people make the mistake of fantasizing about where the relationship is going. This is just the beginning. Don't get ahead of yourself. Just have fun and enjoy.

3. We have to prepare for another scenario. The person we went out with might not call us again, or we may not want them to. Even though we had a good time, sometimes the right chemistry just isn't there. We have to remember that not everyone is *the one*, and rejection isn't the end of the world.

4. The aim of the first or second date is to get to know the other person – to get comfortable with each other and be open to new experiences. The main thing is not to mislead the other person by trying to impress them with who we think they want us to be. Be yourself. Be honest.

5. When you meet someone on the internet, you must be very careful and, again, be truthful. Don't send out a 10 or 20-year-old picture. You are *you*, and you are special and unique in your own way. DON'T start ANY relationship with a LIE. Why waste your time and theirs?

6. Don't think about sex right away. Friendship should come first. Just enjoy meeting this new

person and relax. It's funny, but as we get older, sex is not a comment on our morality, thank God! We don't have to think of it the moment we meet someone. If and when the time comes, you'll be prepared for it.

7. Remember to keep that positive attitude in order to maintain the relationship that could blossom into a beautiful romance.

When you finally find that special someone, how do you keep the relationship alive and flourishing?

1. Spend time together! This could mean talking about things you've been doing or want to do, taking a walk hand in hand, going out for a Sunday afternoon picnic or just sharing time together.

2. Create a connection with one another. By that I mean, be open to affection. How about an impromptu hug or kiss? Be there for each other by listening and truly hearing what the other person is saying. This will give you the chance to open your hearts and minds to one another.

3. Whenever you're with them, remember to always say positive things about them. Wouldn't it be nice to let them know how nice they look or how you enjoyed the movie they chose for you to

see? I know these are just bits of conversation, but little messages of communication create a sense of trust and safety with each other and build respect and pride with the other person.

Lets Talk about Romance

Romance, thank goodness, is alive and well at any age. It's what holds love together. I wonder how many of you think that romance and sex are the same thing. They're not, and here's the difference...

Romance is:
A mental and spiritual feeling which makes your partner feel needed, wanted, and special. It can be fun, light-hearted, mystical, magical, and passionate.

Sex is:
Mostly physical. It can be a lot of work and can end quickly, sometimes with no passion or feeling at all.

Our bodies still crave what everyone else's does. *We are not dead – above or below the waist!* A mature person wants what I call "closeness" in the beginning and during a relationship. Age does not have anything to do with our sexual needs.

Every person is different – our needs are all individual needs. What makes one couple completely happy is totally different from what makes another couple completely happy. So whether it's 2 times, 3 times or 10 times (more or less) that we get together intimately with our significant other, is personal, BUT there should never be a preconceived "number" for when you want to be with each other – just enjoy and feel the excitement and fulfillment you can achieve time and time again. YOUR CALL! – YOUR LIFE! – YOUR CHOICE! – LIVE IT!

You could be having a wonderful, intimate, non-sexual, romantic relationship with a charming partner. Whether it's physical or not, you want to feel a complete sense of satisfaction. This enjoyment comes from holding hands, hugging, kissing, or just sitting and talking till all hours. Having a sexual relationship can be interpreted in many ways. It's not just physical. The physical part of sex sometimes lasts but minutes, but the mental and spiritual connection can bring two people together, and last forever. The type of sex I'm talking about, which I call 'non-sex,' bridges the gap between two mature adults to make a lasting and beautiful bond. The most important thing I'd like to impart is that sex/romance can be the most fabulous and exciting adventure anyone can have, no matter how old or how young they are.

Romance has to start somewhere. It usually begins with the first sight of someone who interests you. That first eye contact – that first look – that first smile – is when the chemistry begins – or doesn't. You think, "Yes, I'd like to meet him or her."

Don't be afraid to say hello first. It's fun to say to someone, "Hi! Love what you're wearing," or "Oh, your dog is so cute!" (even if it's a bulldog). If the person responds, great. If not, MOVE ON. There are a lot of other people out there who will be attracted to you.

What is this thing we call chemistry? I think of it as a flirtatious, fun, exciting moment when two people feel the same kind of energy toward one another.

Keeping the Joy of Romance Alive

Here are a few ideas to keep it going:

1. Do something nice for the other person. Just like that – out of the blue – do it just because you care about them. I remember my Mother telling me that about a year after she got married, at age 16, my Dad, 18, brought her flowers. My mother, being young and a little suspicious, thought my Dad had done something wrong and was making up for it by bringing her flowers. So she said, "What did you do?" My Dad was crushed and even though they were married for 63 years, HE NEVER BROUGHT HER FLOWERS AGAIN! – Remember that when your mate does something special for you, don't ask why, just say thank you.

2. Dress for romance: WOMEN – buy a sexy bra and DON'T go to bed in flannel PJs. MEN – get some satin PJ bottoms – NOT everyday underwear.

3. PLAY, PLAY, PLAY! Take a shower/bath together and maybe massage each other in all the right places. Another benefit of playing together is that it reduces stress and gives you a better night's sleep.

4. Keep the line of communication open and never, ever, go to bed or part angry. Master the art of give-and-take in all situations. In other words, learn to compromise. Choose which battles are important and which ones to let go. Respect and trust one another. Have faith and interest in what the other is doing or wants to do. Each of us wants to be loved. No matter how old, how young or how different we are, we all want to feel that someone truly cares about us. I'm not talking about the love we share with our families and friends. I'm talking about that special person who can truly make the birds sing, the flowers bloom, and the world turn. I love being loved, and I also love to love. But remember to choose wisely and carefully.

5. Work at truly learning about each other's wants, needs and desires. Don't be selfish. If your partner needs something to help stimulate his or her sexual drive, be a part of finding solutions to help them reach sexual satisfaction. If 'toys' are necessary, use them. REMEMBER THE NUMBER "69" (SOIXANTE-NEUF) for it can make two people not only feel completely satisfied but

enjoy the excitement of intimacy without intercourse. Discovering new things about each other is one of the best parts of a true relationship.

Go after what you want. Don't listen to other people saying, "Why would you, at this stage of your life, go out of your way to keep the romance going or find a new one?"
IF NOT NOW, WHEN?

Reaching the Point of No Return

GUESS WHAT? IT'S BEDTIME! In one of my senior sexuality classes, someone asked, "How long should you wait before you go to bed?" If there's chemistry, if there's a feeling of excitement being with that person, go for it now -- WE'RE NOT GETTING ANY YOUNGER! If you wait too long and keep dissecting it (we're not doctors), then the spontaneity that characterizes that part of the romance will be gone. That spontaneity will only last as long as you create it and keep it going.

Your romantic relationship is going to a wonderful, new place: intimacy. You are at the point where you can talk to each other about anything, be happy being together, and need no other company but yourselves.

When I date a gentleman for the first time, I have him pick me up at home, and I always show him around my pink house. When we get to my bedroom and he sees my bed with all the fun pink stuffed animals on it, he will invariably ask: "How in the world does anyone get near that bed?" And I always smile and reply, "With good intentions and lots of money." That's a great way to begin the evening and set boundaries at the same time, but in a fun way!

First things first: Let's look at how one gets into the bedroom...

1. Dating someone for a while (it's up to you to set the time), is going to eventually lead to physical intimacy – unless you just want a friend – in which case, an English Sheepdog is nice to have around!

2. Each of you will have a different time schedule for when you're ready. You'll know it, and so will your partner. Remember, when we reach this fabulous time of 60-plus, in certain instances, one week in our lives is like a month to someone younger.

3. It starts with a kiss. Did you like it? Do you feel any chemistry there? Is the person's kissing exciting to you? Is it giving you "that certain feeling?"

4. Have you begun to touch each other as well as kiss? It's very important to touch the other person. Are you enjoying it? The feeling, touching, kissing can go on for quite a while, but our bodies, our physical reaction to these intimate little moments, will have begun to kick in to our physical needs. Above all, and I know this is in all our minds at this time – please, do not be ashamed of your body. WE ARE WHO WE ARE!

Now, I understand that for many of you it's the first time in a long time that you're even considering being intimate with a new partner. Like me, many of you were married for a number of years. Some have been widows/widowers for just a short time, others for quite a while. Some of you are divorced. Some are in relationships that are having intimacy problems and are not working out. But all of you have feelings of wanting to be close and needed in some way.

When we're dating someone we care about, it naturally puts us in a heightened state of expectation. That's OK. All it means is that we are alive and well and smelling the roses. We should realize by this time in our lives that we will never again be 20, 30, 40 or even 50. Our bodies have changed, but so has our partner's. Get over feeling self-conscious. Don't concern yourself with what *was*. Think about feeling good with what *is*.

Though the frequency of sexual activity may vary as one ages, the amount of sexual interest remains fairly constant. Mae West remarked, "You only live once, but if you do it right, once is enough!"

Even though sexual drive often diminishes with age, there are things that can be done to revive it. There are drugs like Viagra and Cialis for men, and the new PINK pill for women to help boost their sexuality.

Here are some things we should think about:

1. Sexuality is normal, natural and needed in older adults.
2. There is more to sexuality than just intercourse.

3. Although older men and women may have less frequent sexual activity than younger ones, they're not necessarily less content or less satisfied.

4. People who are enjoying satisfying and safe sex – emotionally and physically – are a happier and healthier group.

Statistically, we are finding that the largest group at risk for STDs (sexually transmitted diseases), including HIV (human immunodeficiency virus), are adults over the age of 60. Every one of us has sexual feelings. Don't throw them away on just anybody. BE CHOOSY, BE CAREFUL, and above all, BE SAFE. It's true, we can't get pregnant, but we can get STDs. Hopefully, we'll have learned about the necessity of condoms. So please be careful and practice safe sex.

We also have to acknowledge that we're living in the HIV/AIDS/STD generation. Things might get a bit uncomfortable at this stage in the romance department if one or the other doesn't want to practice safe sex. You have to look at this in an adult manner and decide what's comfortable for both of you.

Considering people are living longer now and enjoying extended sex lives because of hormone therapy and erectile-dysfunction drugs, our generation has to realize the dangers in not practicing safe sex. Many senior health centers are passing out free condoms. Please, please think before having unsafe sex. It's a fact that 60% of all American couples over the age of 50, according to AARP, continue to have sex two or more times a month, with half of those averaging three times a week!

We don't know where our new partners have been or who they've been with. And they don't always remember either. In this day and age, it is most important to talk about safe sex when the time comes.

Here are some questions to ask your potential partner:

1. How many people have you had relations with in the past few years?

2. Depending on the answer to the first question, if you're still truly concerned, there's nothing wrong with asking your partner to take an HIV test.

Today the spread of HIV is rapid in the senior population. Anyone at any age can get the virus that causes AIDS. A joke that's going around is that now grandkids are talking to their grandparents about safe sex. How the tables have turned in the past 50 years! All kidding aside, it's a serious part of a relationship. Our aging population must be able to avoid deadly mistakes, and they could truly be deadly!

The Art of Buying Condoms

While we're on the subject of intimacy, we definitely need a lesson in the art of buying condoms. Did you know that condoms come in all sizes, shapes, colors, thicknesses and a variety of stimulants as well as wild and crazy names?

How do I know this? Let me tell you about my adventure in buying condoms. To be truthful, it was a bit daunting. Having been married 39 years to one man, I had never used a condom. But let me tell you, I got quite an education.

I was giving a seminar on senior sexuality and wanted to talk about condoms and hand out samples to the class. So I went to my local drugstore and asked the young man at the counter, "Where do you keep your condoms?" The look on his face told me that he was shocked at this older woman asking for condoms, but that was only the beginning! He went on to explain that the condoms were locked in a glass cabinet in the back. Turns out there's a secret place where the keys to the *condom kingdom* are held. So I said, "Okay, who's got the key?"

He escorted me to where the condoms were displayed. OMG! I was overwhelmed and surprised by the different names and kinds of condoms that are available… and the packaging. He told me they come in 3's, 6's, 12's and the *family pack* of 36. When he got the cabinet open, I chose many different boxes of assorted condoms. Thinking about my *Senior Sexuality Classes*, I said, "I'll take 3 of the 3 packs, 6 of the 6's, 12 of the 12's and throw in 5 of the family packs!"

After picking the young man's jaw off the floor, I smiled at him as I made my purchase and walked out of the store. I'm sure he went home that evening and told everyone about the "little pink madam" who was stocking up on condoms for her house of ill repute.

It's the best investment you can make for under $10. Some of the names are funny, and some are the traditional ones we've heard for years:

> TROJANS – *sounds like the warriors are "coming" to get us into bed.*

> LOVE – *makes me think of intimacy and romance, like the scene in "From Here to Eternity" where Deborah Kerr is on the beach with Burt Lancaster. My only question is how did they put the condom on while swimming in the ocean?*

> TROPICAL FLAVORS - *sounds like a Mai Tai.*

> *And here's my idea for a new condom:* GOLDEN RODS – *joysticks in a box for mature adults!*

When you're ready for bed and your partner says, "I don't like wearing a condom," or "I would definitely wear one, but I forgot to bring them," guess what you should do? You bring out a handful of condoms and say, "No problem. I'm fully stocked. Your choice!"

The Heat Continues – In Bed

It's now the first time you're going to be intimate with your new partner. The first sexual encounter between you is likely to be awkward until you get to know each other's needs. That's to be expected and quite normal. Learning what your partner expects is the next-best part of the journey in this romantic, sexual encounter. It's all part of the loving.

It's actually an education for both of you. Why not treat it as if it's a game? It can be fun, creative, enjoyable and certainly "entertaining." The reward will be the time you spend exploring ways to please one another. In this game of love, that's what it takes for both of you to be winners. In getting to know one another, the most important factor is to keep it energetic, upbeat, and interesting. This will keep your romance alive and your intimate moments joyous.

I once read that older couples may need 'pillow talk' more than they need pills. That means being honest about your sexual needs. You have to be able to tell each other when things are not right, and be free to correct them. But most important, remember to tell each other when they *are* right.

Yes, there are different ways to be intimate with your new love in these mature years. Some of us will actually enjoy two things. One is the fun and creative imagination of just "playing around" in bed. Many of you like riding a horse; I prefer riding a cowboy! Holding each other, hugging, kissing and touching each other in places that will stimulate sexual feelings is the first part. The second is the actual act of intercourse. Even if there are health issues or physical disabilities, as I've said, there are ways to combat sexual dysfunction by medication, physical therapy and other means.

Many of us at this age cannot achieve the actual act of intercourse... and that's OK. There are many ways

159

to enjoy our partners by being passionate, imaginative and creative in finding new ways to please each other. The art of oral sex, the fun of finding toys to help with stimulation to achieve a climax, are all definitely in the realm of what we can still accomplish at this time.

Talk to each other openly about the things you would like to have happen in bed before the actual act of intercourse. If a man finds it difficult to have an erection, there are many solutions. God bless Viagra, Cialis and penile implants! What a difference they've made in our sex lives! And if a woman is "dry" because of age or when there's not enough foreplay, there are creams and jellies that will help.

We are not children. We are adults. And we are human. By this time in our lives, we've found out, through experience, what we like and don't like. Thank goodness! The ability to talk freely about sex is imperative to all relationships, no matter the age, and the only way to enjoy our intimate moments with our chosen partners is to be who you are in bed AND out of bed – caring, kind, loving and romantic to each other.

Ideas for Romancing the Aging Lover

I think one of the most important things in relationships is to have a good time. A great way to treat your partner to a fun, exciting and passionate day/ evening is to give them a present – a reward.

This reward could be in appreciation of what a wonderful partner they are in every way. A great example: Make up 3 X 5 cards and title them "TIME TO ENJOY."Here are a couple of ideas:

Card #1 might read: "For the one I love. This love reward gives you a 15- minute massage of your choice. Whenever and Wherever." Be careful with this one, my lover chose Starbucks – and now we can never go back to that location ever again!

Card #2 might read: "For the one I love. This love reward entitles you to a night of sexual intimacy your way (if we don't fall asleep first)."

What this does is make our partners aware of how much we appreciate them. It lets them know that just because we don't say it often, doesn't mean we don't care.

You can show someone you love them in a number of ways. Keeping the romance going should not be a chore, but something you want to do naturally. Buying the other person the perfume or cologne they like or a sexy undergarment keeps the romance continually spicy.

Let me tell you something, my friends. Sex can be fun, exciting and interesting. It all depends on how we go about creating romance. We can always learn new things about our significant other, even after many years of living together. It's all about ***exploring*** and ***inventing.***

Throw out the rules!

1. Rearrange your intimate time together, especially if you're retired. Mornings for romantic interludes are not out of the question now, and can sometimes be even more exciting. You're relaxed and you've both had a good night's sleep. So go for it!
2. Learn to flirt again. This goes for both partners. Remember, it takes two to tango. The problem is we get too comfortable with each other. Try calling one another during the day and saying a simple, "LOVE YOU, LOOKING FORWARD TO SEEING YOU SOON." When you're together, a hug and/or a kiss would be delightful.
3. If you're concerned that your body has changed over the years, just put dimmers on your light switches or maybe get some mood lighting. It does wonders for people's psyches!

To find happiness in your life today, just go for it! It's within your grasp if you just take that chance. And that's what life is all about – CHANCE! So take that chance and *GET UP, GET OUT, & GET A LIFE!* while you can still enjoy the ride.

Life's Lessons – All That Glitters Is Not Gold

It's not easy to end a relationship to which we've physically, mentally, and spiritually devoted ourselves. But, sometimes it just doesn't work, no matter what we do or the length of time we've given it. At any age, staying in a committed relationship that's not a happy and contented one can be a detriment to one's physical, mental and spiritual health. Far better to end it and go on with your life with less stress and less pain. And yes, "It's better to have loved and lost than never to have loved at all."

Please, don't ever delude yourself into thinking that the things you dislike about your significant other will change, especially at this time of their life. Believe me when I tell you it hardly ever does.

Once you do decide to end a relationship, don't look back. And, please, do not listen to what other people are telling you to do, because they're not walking in your shoes. Once you make up your mind, move out, move on, and get on with the rest of your life.

When you're faced with a tough decision in your life...

1. Pay attention to how you're feeling. Are you anxious, pressured, depressed, confused or alone? Do your partner's negative points outweigh their positive ones? Make two lists – their Good Points and their Bad Points. Take a realistic look at them. If you can ignore some of the negatives that are causing concern, and see that the positives outweigh them, you'll stand a better chance of making the right decision. But when you do make that decision, do what makes you feel good about yourself.

2. Be mindful of the real reason you're unhappy in the relationship. If you've tried to change things because they truly bother you, but the change isn't happening, don't be fooled. Don't get locked into thinking that tomorrow will be a better day. It's not going to happen. End it! When you make your final decision, do it. Think about your happiness. Remember, you were alone before you met that person, and you managed. Your life will go on to find that special someone... and so will theirs.

If you finally make up your mind to leave, don't let anyone change it. Stop thinking, " How can I leave at this time in my life? What will people say? It's not right or fair." It's not right or fair to whom? It's certainly not right or fair to you. Stop thinking that way!

What happens is that a lot of past guilt starts to come up from deep inside you. You MUST let it go! Lose it, for guilt will only keep you in a relationship that will eventually bring you down. At this stage and age in your life, you want to be able to live without anger, fear, resentment, or unhappiness. When you leave a bad relationship, I know that you will feel free and at peace with yourself once again.

It isn't easy. Life isn't easy. But when you open up your heart again, you will be giving your soul a chance to sing, dance, cry and laugh on YOUR OWN TERMS, not anyone else's.

If you've truly done your part, but your partner wants to break up with you, or you with them, so be it. It was probably not meant to be anyway. As the old expression goes, "C'est la vie!" (That's life!) I say, *Get Up, Get Out & Get a New Life!* For at this time, why would you want to waste these precious moments? Why waste your energy and love on someone who doesn't give a damn and who's not willing to make you happy? You will find Mr./Ms. Right when you're healthy, happy, and content with who you are. If you're NOT where you want to be, then it's time to move out and move on with your life.

Remember, sex is a good exercise, but love is a better one. Choose carefully. Think about who will give you the most for your time. Remember that relationships are like flowers. Some are good for only a few days; others keep blooming. Choose wisely. Finding happiness in later years takes time, courage, and a passion to make it happen.

When we move on, we have to learn what to be grateful for in our lives. So remember, always start by seeing the best in yourself; for you are number one. The relationship that matters most is the one you have with yourself. Feeling good about who you are is the key factor in making any relationship a success.

Let's continue on our journey to *Get a Life,* and believe, with all our hearts, that to love and be loved is a gift that's out there for all of us to enjoy and embrace. And don't forget:

SENIOR SEXUALITY IS ALIVE AND WELL...

ANY TIME
ANY PLACE
AND AT ANY AGE!

Section Four
GET A LIFE!

Life Isn't About Finding Yourself
Life Is About Creating Yourself

The Best of Times Is NOW

I believe that the key to growing older is to do everything we can NOT to hold back time, but rather, make time work for us. The key to this is learning to enjoy our lives at this moment; for it is today, now, this very second that is truly important to all of us.

MAKE THE BEST OF THE TIME YOU HAVE. Life at this stage is definitely challenging, and at the same time, adventurous and exciting.

I believe that we can be advocates – at this time in history – to change the world's perception of what the older generation is and can be. At age 60 and up, we continue to have the capability and experience to do our jobs productively and creatively.

I see even now that the world is beginning to recognize what's happening to our age group. Now that the Baby Boomers are coming into our generation, suddenly all the major brand-name products are age-conscious – from cosmetics to nutritional foods, television programs, clothing and travel. The corporate world wants your business and with the help of the Boomers, we are changing the way corporate America sees us.

You remember the Baby Boomers? They were the ones who started the sit-ins and the love-ins in the 1960s. But most important, they were the ones who embraced rebellion in all forms with passion and conviction. THEY WILL DO THE SAME THING ABOUT AGING.

Guess what? We all look like big dollar signs. All the marketers are suddenly realizing that our generation has the disposable income and the time to buy and use their products. Those of us who are already in our golden years would be wise to join forces with them to become the number one economical, political, social, and spiritual group in today's world. I am proud to be part of this growing group who will never grow old – just older. One could say that the new mature adult doesn't really ever retire, but continues to evolve.

So my dear contemporaries, let's enjoy being new-age adults. We know we're not going to live forever, but while we're here, we're not going to waste time lamenting about what could have been, but continue to look forward to what will be. Let's make our new mantra *Get Up, Get Out, & Get a Life!*

I say it's never, ever too late to RESTART, RETHINK and REINVENT your life. Make sure you give yourself a chance by setting your mind in a positive mode to "let the good times roll." I like the line: "The best way we can predict the future is to create it ourselves."

Think about what you would like to do, then think of where you could go for ideas about how to accomplish it. It's a fact that by shedding old ideas, you can create a brighter and more energized way of life. Clinging to old, irrelevant things or beliefs holds you back. It confines you to spaces that no longer fit what you want in your new life. So shed your old skin and transform yourself into the NEW YOU!

Don't limit yourself. We all have the power to open ourselves up to change. Use it! Think of yourself as a sponge to absorb all the good things that are out there like meeting new people, enjoying new relationships and traveling new roads. Accept and appreciate who and what you are, and make sure you keep yourself young in spirit by holding onto your dreams.

The key is to be confident in who you are. Give yourself the opportunity to reinvent yourself. And when you do, it will be easy to *Get Up, Get Out,* and finally *Get a Life* that you will truly enjoy living. It's never too late to start a new life or find gratification with the one you have.

We all have a story to tell. Remember, it's not how we *tell* that story, but how we *live* it. I love proving every day of my life that age is only a number. Who's to say what you or I can or cannot accomplish? Who's to say that life has to slow down or pass you by when you've reached a certain age?

Ways to Reach for and Grab Hold of the Stars

1. Accept yourself. Stop being your own worst critic and start being your own best friend. Appreciate who and what you are.
2. Make sure you laugh your way through life's changes. Tears happen. Endure, grieve, and learn to move on.
3. Seize the day. Do something new, no matter how small it is, that gives each day a purpose.
4. As you age, you can still be vital, exciting, productive, and definitely sexy. Give yourself the opportunity to reinvent yourself and promote the new you.
5. It is important that you learn to renew and deepen your spiritual faith. Keep away from the words, "I cannot, I should not, I must not." One of the worst things we can do is procrastinate. Make sure you follow through on the important things that will make you happy and comfortable.

At this time in our lives, I believe it is important to revitalize, recommit, and renew our spirits as we journey on the road to reinventing ourselves. Think of all the positive energy out there and do yourself a favor by opening your mind to gather it in. Learn to live healthier and longer by realizing that your life can still be useful and meaningful.

Why are you taking the time to read this book? I truly hope and pray that it is to open yourself to a new realm of possibilities; to change and reinvent how you feel and how you live. Ask yourself, "Am I still growing? Am I still finding new and exciting adventures in my life? Am I happy and content with where I am?" If you're not satisfied with the answers that you're getting, you need to change your outlook on how you're living. You need to redefine who you are in order to be able to continue to grow. Why? Because WHEN YOU STOP GROWING, YOU STOP LIVING.

You must always be the master of your own emotions, for only you can control the way you feel and how you act. It's all about your attitude and gratitude, and how you use it. Starting over at our stage in life is not only possible, it's being done everyday by people like you and me. This is the real world. Age is a chronological statistic, but youthfulness is a state of mind. The great thing about getting older is that you don't ever lose all the other ages you've been.

I truly believe it's worth the effort to *Get Up, Get Out, & Get a Life!* You are beginning a personal journey. You may be a little uncertain about where you're going, but if you learn to stand on your own two feet, your legs will get stronger and they'll be able to take you up that road to new adventures.

Yes, there may be mistakes along the way. It happens to all of us. Take the time to learn from these mistakes and try not to be too hard on yourself. You are making your own choices. You're embarking on a road of discovery by being:

1. *Confident in your own skin and in your own mind*
2. *Knowledgeable about what works and what doesn't work for you*
3. *Courageous and passionate enough to achieve your goals*

You don't spend 60-plus years on this earth without learning how to carefully ponder your next move. But sometimes you've got to do what you've got to do – right here/right now – by saying to yourself, "You know what? To hell with it! I'm going to do what I want to do in my own way and in my own time!"

Who's to say life has to slow down? NOT ME! Let's stay the course and concentrate on living, loving and laughing our way through these best years we still have. Choose your battles wisely. Pick the ones that are really important to you. Don't make excuses. You're far too *young* and bright for that.

Willpower and patience are the keys that allow you to *Get Up, Get Out, & Get a Life*! If you have the will, if you want things to change, you will find a way – just be patient with yourself. Remember what I said: "Don't let anyone rain on your parade."

Today let's fall in love
with the person in the mirror,
the one you see every day
but seldom truly look at,

172

the one who gives more
than he or she ever takes.
Today let's take nothing,
not this day, not this moment,
not this chance, not even ourselves
for granted.
Let's first love who we are.

The Art of Reinvention

"It's all about me" is NOT a selfish statement, but a true and honest way of thinking about reinventing yourself in order to enjoy this time in your life. We should feel comfortable in our own bodies and confident in our own special creative abilities.

Let's talk about how anyone who wants to change something in their lives can absolutely do it. We really have so much to be grateful for. First, and most obvious, is that we're still here, alive and kicking. So let's live this day, this week, this month and this year as if it were a gift – a true "present" to enjoy.

In reinventing our lives, we have to do what we feel we can do. It's not really that difficult, but it does take courage. Don't make the mistake of saying, "One day I'll do that... Someday I'm going to try that..."

BIG MISTAKE! For that day may never come.

Live for today!

What you are doing takes real courage…

Courage is the feeling that you can make it,
no matter how challenging the situation.
It is knowing that you can reach out for help
and you are not alone.
Courage is accepting each day,
knowing that you have the inner resources
to deal with the ordinary things
as well as the confusing things;
with the exciting things
as well as the painful things.
Courage is taking the time to get involved
with life, family, and friends,
and giving your love and energy
in whatever ways you can.
Courage is being who you are,
being aware of your good qualities and talents,
and not worrying about what you do not have.
Courage is allowing yourself to live
as fully as you can,
to experience as much of life as you are able to,
to grow and develop yourself
in whatever directions you need to.
Courage is having hope for the future
and trust in the natural flow of life.
It is being open to change.
Courage is having faith
that life is a beautiful gift.

~ *Donna Levine Small*

My First Times Alone

It takes courage and the inner conviction that we're doing the right thing. We must believe in ourselves. We must believe that we can do whatever we set out to do, and make that belief part of our lives. Everyday you're learning to make choices to please yourself, not anyone else.

When I think of all the firsts in my life, I naturally think of my first date, my first marriage and my first child. But then there comes a time, after many years, through circumstance we become alone, and we have to start all over, making decisions on our own.

I can remember soon after my husband died, I needed to replace my car. OH MY GOD, talk about courage… It took me days to get up enough courage to go to the dealership. I didn't want to ask my children for help as I wanted to prove to them (and to myself) that I could be independent and in complete control.

As I entered the dealership, I was approached by one of many people who were there to, supposedly, "help me buy a car." Thank goodness, I had come prepared! I knew exactly what kind of car I wanted, exactly what I wanted in it, exactly what color I wanted and exactly the price I wanted to pay. I told the person that I knew there were a lot of steps to buying a car, but I only wanted to talk to the last person, the one who had final approval, to sell me a car that day.

I was turned over to a gentleman, Max, who thought that he was going to sell me the Taj Mahal: He started to go through a hundred different ways the car

175

could come. I said, "STOP," and handed him a piece of paper with exactly what I wanted. I had done my homework. When he tried to continue I exclaimed, "I'm giving you five minutes to write up a contract MY WAY or I'm walking."

He got the message, but when I looked at the final contract, it listed an additional $50 for putting on my license plates. I told him that I could get a screwdriver and do it myself, except I was not going to break my nails. "So take it OFF," I insisted. Within an hour, I had my new car – with license plates attached *at no cost and no broken nails.*

There are many firsts that occur when we are alone. Like the first time you go to a fancy restaurant alone, or when you travel by yourself. So I say to all of you – just remember that YOU CAN DO IT when you believe and trust in yourself. So celebrate your own uniqueness and individuality.

Someone once stated, "There was a time when I couldn't see the road ahead. So I hit the accelerator, and the whole world opened up for me." How true that is!

What does *reinvent* really mean? How does one do it? In my case, I just said to myself, "What have I got to lose? Nothing!" After all, age is only a number, and when you add all the numbers together they equal *wise!* I want you to forget the words *old* and *aging.* Instead, I suggest you use *mature, seasoned,* and *experienced.* I like the sound of those much, much better.

Getting a new life sometimes means we have to vacate the place we've called home for many years. But things happen. That's life. At this point, some of us need to give our minds, bodies and spirits room to grow in a different environment from our past comfort zones. It's redefining ourselves and making changes. I remember a line from a play I was in that sums it all up: "If not now… when?"

I'm tired of people who feel they're being kind or that they're protecting me when they try to limit what I want to do. I continue to feel that I'm in my prime. If I don't move my body, if I don't use my brain, if everyone else does things for me, I will become helpless – physically, emotionally and spiritually. We need to tell everyone around us to let us do whatever we think we're capable of accomplishing. If we need help, if we want help, we'll ask for it.

The time is now. The 60-plus generation will leave a legacy by igniting a true and positive revolution in the reinvention of themselves and America. Today there are infinite ways to reinvent ourselves. We have more time, more energy and more knowledge with which to change the way America and the world think about getting older.

We can transform healthcare, create secure retirement, and build better communities for older adults that will preserve their dignity and well-being. We will also be able to revitalize the workplace so that mature adults will be viewed as the assets they are and be able to remain productive at their jobs many years beyond the prescribed retirement age.

A popular song in the 60's was Bob Dylan's *The Times They Are a- Changin*. It's no different today. Times are changing at a faster and more furious pace than ever before. And with this time, we can make a difference! We are at a unique moment in history when the need for change and the demand for new lifestyles and more creativity are coming together. The time for reinvention is now. The moment is upon us. Grab hold of it and ride it through.

Reinvention Is Not Just a Word

Reinvention can make your world a better place. By developing your own personality, look, and style, and by setting your own rules and believing in your own inner spirit, you will sleep better, eat healthier and breathe easier. You'll walk with more confidence and greater freedom of movement. When this happens, you will become your own true free spirit again.

The power to achieve this is within you when you have the right attitude and the feeling of gratitude. It is the belief that you can, and the knowledge that you're *THE ONLY ONE* who can make these changes to your life. The question is, are you willing to change? Are you willing to take the risk of changing your attitude and your lifestyle?

In writing this book, I hope to show you that it's possible to achieve your goals and be able to reinvent your life. It's what I call a 'mind shift.' It doesn't have to be on the stroke of midnight that one changes the way they do things. You can begin to get the life you love and be able to live it any time you choose.

The key is to get motivated. It starts with believing that you can do whatever you want. Take time to think about what's important to you at this stage of your life. Think about the goals and areas you want to change, modify or add to. Here are a few things you can do to help get started:

1. Establish a support system. Find a group of like-minded people who can help you develop and keep your goals on track.
2. Review your commitments, prioritize them, and focus on the ones you want to accomplish first.
3. Remember, nothing is easy. Everything takes effort and courage, but the outcome far outweighs any negative forces that might slow you down.
4. Learn to be patient, kind, and gentle with yourself, and don't take life so seriously that you forget to enjoy the journey.
5. It's never too late or too early to have a new life experience. This is, after all, your life. Live it! Love it! And, for better or worse, hold onto it! As the saying goes, "we do not stop playing because we grow old; we grow old because we stop playing."

Choosing an upbeat outlook on life is a philosophy that all of us can and should embrace. To start on the right path, repeat these "mantras" aloud every day:

1. I will have positive expectations for everything I do.
2. I will surround myself with positive people and attitudes.

3. I will not dwell on past failures, but only think of future successes and keep trying until I achieve the positive results I want.

When you reinvent your life, the first thing you need to do is remove any unhealthy obstacles that are keeping you from enjoying it. Discard those things from the past that have stopped you from becoming the person you really want to be. Now, make a list of things you want to focus on at this time. Maybe you've always wanted to change your look, travel more, be more active, meet new people, or even write a book (like I did.) Make that happen now. Start with the easy changes and build up from there. Find the life you want and live it. *You deserve it!*

The reality is that there are thousands of people out there like you and me who are reinventing themselves every day. Reinvention is not a trend. It's a complete personal revolution. This is a generational movement that echoes what's happening in our world today.

The desire to accomplish something new requires that we have the motivation, determination and commitment to that goal. I'm totally aware that this is not always an easy step to take. I've been there. At 72, I thought I was way too old to start to reinvent myself. How wrong I was! We can all make this the biggest, most exciting, most satisfying time of our lives. It is possible, it is plausible, and it is pleasurable. But it will take time. It doesn't happen overnight.

Time, as we get older, becomes more precious. It's not unusual for us to think about our mortality and whether we have enough time to reinvent ourselves. I say we do. We've worked long and hard to reach this point, so why not be able to enjoy life and live it to the max no matter what age we are? Happiness can be achieved when we consistently move toward what is really important to us.

The Other "R" Words

Positive attitudes are definitely helping mature adults live much longer and healthier lives. We must understand that one does get older, but the way in which we get older determines how we will live the rest of our time here on Earth.

Get over being unhappy or unsatisfied with who you are. You are YOU! If you want to change, it's never *ever* too late to REINVENT, RETHINK, REBUILD and RENEW your life.

It took time to reinvent myself, as I was trying to please everyone except the one person I should have been trying to please: ME! I finally came to the realization that this is *my* time, Jackie's time, Pink Lady's time. I decided I was going to live my life the way I've always wanted by rediscovering and revitalizing my zest for living life to the fullest. I set my heart and mind to use my physical body, my spiritual soul and my life-long emotional experiences to get the most out of these beautiful, vital and exciting years of my life. This is, after all, our last hurrah... MAKE THE MOST OF IT!

We all set different goals for ourselves. Each of us will achieve them to different degrees. They are all possible, but in the end, the most important thing is that they'll bring us the happiness we so well deserve. The main thing to remember is that we are all in a *doing* pattern, not just a *holding* pattern.

It is time for a BRAND-NEW YOU!

REINVENT your own fabulous and creative ideas.
REDISCOVER your own potential and inner strengths.
REJOICE in who you are and who you will become.

Fabulous at Any Age – The Senior Pageant

A year after Walter died, I started dating. I attended a singles event called *Seniors Still Out There*. There, I met a very nice gentleman who had been a producer and director in the film industry for many years. It was he who pointed me toward my next big adventure, by suggesting that I would be a fantastic contestant for a *Ms. Senior Pageant* he had heard about. My response was (talk about attitude), "You're out of your mind. I don't do pageants." He finally convinced me that it would be a good way for me to start to *Get a Life*.

So I checked out all the rules and regulations for the Ms. Senior Pageant. The first thing I had to do was send in my picture and my philosophy of life, which the rules stated had to be 32 seconds in length – no more, no less. It did sound kind of easy and fun. So I entered into the spirit of the pageant.

That's when I first wrote my philosophy of life which has been with me ever since...

> *"My philosophy of life is to "THINK PINK" – to feel the energy and the aura of beauty that a color can give to people by seeing life through "rose-colored glasses." It makes living, loving and laughing a beautiful way of life. Whoever comes in contact with this color shares the philosophy that to "think pink" is to see love and inner beauty in everything and everyone around them. It has given me a chance to share this passion with my family, my friends and my community, making this world a better place to live in."*

With that, the committee loved it and invited me into the contest. The contestants in this Ms. Senior L.A. County Pageant ranged in age from 62 to 93. I was only 73 at the time. I knew nothing about pageants. The only thing I knew for sure was that I'd need an evening gown. So I went out and bought the material and had one made. Guess what color it was?

It was a very sweet looking gown, with long sleeves, showing very little cleavage – like something one would wear to their senior prom. Wow! When I

saw the gowns the other contestants were wearing…
talk about shock factor!

There were 23 contestants, all lovely and talented
ladies. The talent included opera singers, a 93-year-old
tap dancer, a salsa dancer, a jazz singer, a variety of
other acts, and a little pink blond who couldn't sing or
dance – me.

There are three parts to the Ms. Senior Pageant.
The first is an interview with five judges, where you're
required to tell them all about yourself, your family,
and why you think you're qualified to win the contest.
For this part of the pageant, I wore a lovely two-piece
suit – very classic and ladylike. What color do you think
that was?

One of the judges was from a major bank in
California. When it was his turn, he asked me, in a very
negative tone, "What is this thing with pink?" Without
hesitating, I replied, "It was a million-dollar marketing
tool, and if your big company was smart, they'd have
tools like this to make more money." I thought, *there it
goes… I'll never get a good grade from this judge!* I later
found out he gave me a top score.

The next phase of the contest is talent. Now, as
I've said, I don't really sing or dance, but my speaking
skills are excellent, so I decided to do a fun monologue
– a variation on Shakespeare's famous speech from
Hamlet. So I began…

To be or not to be… that is the question.
Wrong! The real question is:
To age or not to age… THAT is the question.

Whether 'tis nobler in the mind to suffer the slings and arrows of wrinkles and lines or Botox them, to combat the whips and scorns of aging. Let's all agree that age is only a number... NO MORE. No more sitting around and doing nothing. 'Tis far better to enjoy the freedom of living the best years of our lives to the fullest degree.

Let's keep anger, jealousy, and hate out of our lives, and instead bring in joy, hope and a positive attitude for living out our golden years. You out there... this is no time to call it quits. It's a time to embrace life and all the exciting opportunities it can offer you.

So... Get Up, Get Out, & Get a Life... and make of it what you will. For you are as young as you feel. Remember, it's not when we age, but how we age. Surround thyself with thine own vibrant spirit, and put that energy to work helping yourself and those around you.

At this time in our lives, it's fun and exciting to be our own person, and to create our own style. This is the true key to making these years the most productive ones, and to do it with grace, beauty and dignity.

So, Mr. Shakespeare, in answer to your age-old question, "To be or not to be?" I will be. I will

Get Up, Get Out and start a new chapter of my life. I will enjoy these best years of my life by living, loving and laughing my way through, and remembering to do it in my own ageless style.

Remember, "To age or not to age?" is a question that only you can answer, so come celebrate with me. Be positive. Be outgoing, and make this time of your life count. Make the answer to the questions "To be or not to be?" and "To age or not to age?" a loud and clear response for everyone around you to hear.

I received a lot of applause and felt that the audience was really with me. On with the pageant! Phase three was parading around the stage in our gowns, showing off our poise and grace. Now, I haven't mentioned this before, but in heels I'm a tall 5 feet and barely 90 pounds. My lovely competitors, on the other hand, were all from 5'-3" to 5'-9" and each built like a brick shit house! Their dresses were drop-dead gorgeous, with tons of beading, slits up the wazoo, and lots of cleavage. There was definitely nothing left to the imagination, and here I was in my little pink evening gown, covered up, with no boobs and no legs showing, and nary a bead in sight. I just wanted to hide! I wanted to disappear, but there was an audience of over 750 people waiting to see who we were and what we had to offer.

After two and half hours, the competition was over. We were lined up on the stage, according to height, waiting for the announcement of the winner. As you can guess, I was the last one in line, closest to the wings. And we were all wearing body mics, which, at this point, I had completely forgotten.

As they began to announce the winners, I looked out into the universe, and said to myself, "Thank you, whoever is out there guiding my life. I am proud that I have the *chutzpa*, (courage and boldness) to *Get Up and Get Out* and perform in front of all of these people at this age."

They called out the names of the winners, beginning with the third runner- up. Before they announced the winner, I had already started to edge my way off the stage, assuming that there was no way I had won. As I stepped off the stage onto the stairs, the voice of the judge boomed, "And the winner of our Ms. Senior L.A. County Pageant is our very own energetic and enthusiastic... Pink Lady!"

Forgetting that I had a microphone on, I yelled, "Oh shit!" Then I turned around and ran to the front of the stage where everyone in the audience, by that time, was on their feet simultaneously cheering and laughing.

I spoke to the judges afterward and asked why they had selected me. They answered that they usually voted for singers or dancers, but they all felt that I exemplified the "total package" of what a Ms. Senior should be: *someone with energy, a zest for life, and a fabulous personality.*

It just goes to show what a wonderful world there is out there when you believe in yourself. You can accomplish something that you've never done before, and reach your goals. So here I was... Ms. Senior L.A.

County 2005, and thrilled to death that I had come so far in such a short time. After I'd won the pageant, my friends and family were absolutely convinced that I had done the right thing by putting myself out there... and *so was I*.

People are always asking me how I became who I am today. I don't mind sharing my answers, though I do tell them that my way might not be the way they would go about reinventing themselves. But I'm more than happy to give you a few things to think about:

1. Are you willing to, and do you really want to change? I did. So many people think they do and then realize that they're happy where they are. And that's okay. I knew I had enough of the garment business after almost 40 years, and that time was "not on my side." So I thought of what I could do to make me happy, busy and productive for the next cycle of my life, God willing.

2. How far are you willing to go to change some of your attitudes, your lifestyle and your old ideas? Are you willing to be honest with who you are today and see that a change is needed? With my positive attitude, I knew I was ready to take a chance and add new chapters to my life. I was ready and open to try a completely different life; the one I finally chose was in the entertainment field. I knew that I had nothing to lose. BUT, I did have a lot to gain by starting a new and exciting life. I could now travel, experience uncharted

roads and find a new world that would make the fourth quarter of my life unlike anything I had ever known – thus enabling me to reach new heights in my Golden Years.

3. Are you willing to listen to advice and take the necessary chances to help make a new you possible? I knew I wanted to reinvent myself and that taking chances would be a vital part of the challenge.

Get A Life! Seminars

I believe that everyone should have something they enjoy doing and are passionate about. In my case, I also wanted to be able to help others see life through rose-colored glasses. So I decided to start a company called *Get Up, Get Out, & Get a Life!* to help Baby Boomers and seniors reinvent themselves with a positive attitude. The way I accomplished this was by starting to give motivational seminars that were uplifting and helped define ways that one can change their life with the right attitude.

That decision has taken me on a fantastic journey and has given me the chance to help others enrich their lives. Having a positive attitude and a sense of humor allows me to laugh at and with myself, and has enabled me to have a life that I am proud to live.

Life is not just about what you have *now,* but, as I've said, it's what you do *now* with the life you have that counts. I'm here for the long run and, hopefully, so are you. It's an absolute joy for me when I see people of all ages come together and relish this wondrous journey called life. I tell everyone *"that life is not measured by the number of breaths we take, but by the moments that take our breath away."*

In some of my *Get Up, Get Out, & Get a Life!* Seminars, we talk about the losses that occur in our lives and the choices we have to cope with them. But remember, age has nothing to do with these losses – for it can happen at any age. There are people of all ages who are making the same choices about life as we are.

After I won the pageant, local newspapers began picking up stories about me. That led to the opportunity for me to give motivational classes for seniors at Kaiser Hospital and also teach a series of classes at Pierce College. I started getting speaking engagements at churches, synagogues, Rotary Clubs, senior centers and retirement homes. Some of the subjects covered in my workshops include:

1. The Pros & Cons of Aging (check the alternatives; there are ONLY pros)
2. Negative to Positive/People, Relationships, Family & Friends
3. Words for the Already Wise
4. Dating, Commitment & Finding a Soul Mate
5. Senior Sexuality
6. Laughing Is the Key Ingredient to Happiness

Here is one of my favorite stories that always gets a laugh from my audiences…

A lady walks into a drug store and tells the pharmacist that she needs some cyanide.

"Why in the world do you need cyanide?" the pharmacist asks. The lady then explains that she needs it to poison her husband.

The pharmacist's eyes grew wide… "Lord, have mercy! I can't sell you cyanide to kill your husband! That's against the law! They'll throw us both in jail, and I'll lose my license!"

The lady then reaches into her purse and pulls out a photo of her husband in bed with the pharmacist's wife and hands it to him.

The pharmacist looked at the picture and calmly replied, "Well, you didn't tell me you had a prescription…"

In my seminars I talk about my "pink" house. After people started hearing about my house, they all wanted to come and see it. So I thought it would be a good idea to do some of the workshops in my home and make it a fun event as well.

I can accommodate groups of up to 50 people in my studio. We start with a full breakfast at 10 a.m. Then I give a tour as I tell stories about the pink house. During the tour, I open some of my cabinets, revealing boxes and boxes of pink Kleenex and pink toilet tissue, and closets full of pink clothes, pink shoes and pink accessories.

Having fun at a Get a Life Seminar

In the kitchen, I show them lovely pink pots and pans (that have never been used, since I joke that I really don't cook). In the living room there's a pink car with none other than a pink Raggedy Ann doll sitting at the wheel. As you know, Raggedy Ann dolls are usually dressed in red, white and blue. Not in my house! In my bathroom, the white walls are decorated with pink hearts, and across one of the walls, in bold letters, is written "The Pink Lady."

After the tour, I give a talk on "Being Fantastic at Any Age" and how one has to learn that life is for the living. By the time the workshop concludes at noon, every one of my guests is completely immersed and in love with the color pink. They realize that what I'm telling them is truly what I'm living every day.

The total time they spend in my home and garden is two hours. Everyone has a delightful time, and they all tell their friends about it, which leads to additional events. I have had a number of repeat visitors.

It's funny how people react to my seminars. In one of the classes I gave in my home, the group ranged from 60 to 90 years of age. Three quarters of them were widowed or divorced. About 20 minutes into my talk about relationships, a lady named Esther, who was 79, raised her hand and asked, "Tell me, Pink, do you really date?" With a smile I said, "Of course I do. Do I look like I'm friggin' dead?" Everyone laughed.

A few minutes later Esther's hand went up again. In a hesitant voice, she asked, "Do you... I mean, do you... you know?" Then she stopped. The room went silent. You could hear a pin drop. All ears were tuned in. I laughed and said, "Do you want to know if I have intimate, romantic relations?" She nodded her head, and by now, the entire group was on the edge of their seats. I smiled and asked, "How do I look?" They all answered, "Wonderful, great, beautiful..." Then I asked, "How's my complexion?" "Oh," the woman said, "It's gorgeous." I answered, "Does that answer your question?" With that, the entire room broke into a roar of laughter.

My passion is devoting my life to re-educating people all over the country that being a mature adult over 60 does NOT mean that one is unproductive. IT'S JUST THE OPPOSITE. Our minds, bodies and spirits are eternally young and teeming with the excitement and enthusiasm that we all should have at any age.

Hollywood Calls - A Star Is Born

I was enjoying my Ms. Senior LA County reign and having a great time speaking to people about how this time of their lives can be truly fabulous. An article about my winning the pageant, which carried my picture, was in papers all over L.A. County. A talent agent, Steve Stevens, Sr., saw it and called me into his office for an interview. He asked me to bring a headshot. I didn't have one, so I asked around and found a good photographer who took several great shots. I found Mr. Stevens to be a very professional and knowledgeable agent with a great sense of humor.

During our conversation, I learned that he was one of the original Mouseketeers and knew everyone in Hollywood. He and his son, Steve Stevens, Jr., have proven to be honest and most sincere. Over the past couple of years, Steve, Sr. and his lovely wife, Rosemary, have become very dear friends and are a true example of what a theatrical family can really be – warm, sensitive, caring, helpful and very professional.

When I arrived at his office for that first interview, I handed him my brand-new headshot. He said, "Jackie, let me allay any fears you might have about show business. You don't have to worry about a thing. There are no more casting couches in Hollywood." Hearing that, I immediately grabbed my picture from his hand and said, "Wait a minute! That's why I wanted to get into the business at this age!" With that, Steve laughed and said, "My dear, Jackie, with your personality and fun attitude, you will definitely make it in this town."

My first audition was my most frightening. Here I was, 75 and, in my mind, already a "star!" I was very lucky that the casting agent was as nice as she was, for when she asked me to "slate" I thought she wanted me to write something, and I asked her for a pencil. She smiled and explained that to "slate" is part of the audition process. It means that you stand in front of the camera and say your name with a lot of energy and enthusiasm.

Then she asked me to knock on a door like Jack Nicholson did in *The Shining*. I hadn't seen the movie, but instead of admitting that and asking for clarification, I made my BIG mistake. I went right ahead and knocked on the door as if I were a sweet Avon Lady and in a very kind and polite voice said, "I'm back!"

Now, as I'm sure you know, the character I was supposed to portray was a crazed killer. Needless to say, my nice-lady voice didn't get me that job, but I did learn a lot that day. You must ALWAYS ask questions. They are ALL important. I realized then that *if you do not ask, you do not learn.*

At another of my early auditions I got cast as a little old lady swimming in a pool. Because I wasn't a member of Screen Actors Guild at that time, they were willing to "Taft-Hartley" me into the union. That means that I'd have the right to join the union after the film was completed. I did join, and it was one of the proudest moments of my life (it is now called SAG-AFTRA.

I figured that now that I was in the union, I'd better start taking some acting classes! There are hundreds of acting coaches in and around Hollywood. At that time, I was interested in being in commercials. Where to start? I asked a few people. The name that kept coming up was Buddy Powell. Being a commercial star himself, he is able to teach us to be who we are and also become the character of a real person in a commercial.

Buddy's classes are directed mainly toward people in my age range – the over 60 crowd. He knows exactly what's necessary to help us be successful in the commercial world. But most important at our age, Buddy has the patience and knowledge to steer us in the right direction – and he is a good friend as well as our teacher.

In fact, the very first national commercial I got was during that time in Buddy's class. It was so me! It was a bank commercial, and I was the wife of one of the bankers. The banker was going to commit suicide because business was so bad and I was yelling, "Don't jump, Harry! Who's going to pay for my Botox?" I had more fun on that shoot... everyone said I sounded and looked like the late Joan Rivers.

Many other auditions came my way and I successfully landed some of them. They included a national commercial for Loctite which aired during the 2015 Super Bowl; some TV episodes; a few small films; and lots of theatre. Among a few Southern California

196

public service announcements, was one for the Department of Water and Power that played for over three years on the Metro Bus System in Los Angeles. To this day, people stop me on the street, saying, "Hey, Pink Lady, I saw you on the bus!" I continue to have a fun time auditioning and working, but I do have to confess something. If given my choice, live theatre wins out over film. I love the energy that I get from an audience when I step out on stage and perform.

There is a picture of me in a pink fur coat and a Victoria's Secret teddy that was taken during my very first stage appearance, in *Grapes and Raisins,* at the Stage Door Playhouse. I played the very sexy girlfriend of the male lead. Talk about attitude! When I auditioned for the part, the first thing they asked me was, would I wear sexy lingerie on stage at my age. I looked at the director, laughed and said, "Are you kidding? I can't wait!" Between us, I did *fix up* the costume a little and covered the parts that I didn't think needed to be exposed.

Another example of how a positive attitude can win points in the entertainment field is when I went for an audition a few months ago for the role of an older lady talking to her five-year-old granddaughter. I walked in, and the casting directors were all under 30. One of them said, "I think you're in the wrong place. We're looking for a grandmother type." And I said, "Here I am!"

Now, I'm 84, as you know, but I have always done everything and anything to keep looking young and in shape. That's who I am. It's important to me to always look my best whether I'm at home, out shopping or in a show. I've always maintained the look of a woman who definitely *knows how to Get Up, Get Out, & Get a Life!*

At the audition, though they said I did well, I was left with the impression that they didn't think I was right for the part. A month later, I got a surprise call from the director, who said, "Jackie, we'd like you for the part of the grandmother. And, just for your information, you definitely changed our minds about how a grandmother of today looks and acts!" I was thrilled to pieces to be able to change the young director's stereotypical way of thinking about what today's grandparents look like.

I have taken many acting classes over the past few years, but I remember the very first serious one I took to be in film. I recall going into the class with about 25 others. The teacher had been a famous character actor in his day. For some unknown reason, I thought that I was already a star.

When he handed me a script to read with him, I began with enthusiasm and energy. By the second line I heard him say "STOP. Jackie, take it down a little." I started again and after the first sentence he yelled "STOP. Please, Jackie, take it down a little more." OOOOOkay, I thought to myself. So I took it down. After a few lines, the teacher, in a loud booming voice, interrupted once again, "PLEASE, PLEASE, TAKE IT DOWN."

By now I was in tears, frustrated, and embarrassed. I offered, "But if I take it down anymore, I won't be acting." And the teacher replied, "My dear Jackie, that is what I mean, because *then* you will be real – *and not acting!*

When I started my second career in acting and motivational speaking, some of my so-called friends questioned my reinventing myself. "I don't believe that I can ever retire" I told them. "I don't want to just play cards, watch television or go to the movies. I want to continue to do things that keep my mind, body and spirit alive and active."

I enjoy *the art of networking* with not only my audiences, but with everyone I meet. To engage in conversation with others and make new friends, both in and out of the entertainment field, is what I love to do. And, giving out my pink business cards has become my number one way of connecting with everyone I meet.

Rockin' With the Ages

> *Artistic expression may be the greatest aging antidote ever created.*
> ~ Stuart Kandell, Positive Aging

Throughout this book, I've written about the different stages of my life and all the fantastic adventures I've had up to this point. But my journey, as you will see, is just beginning! In 2008, I created a musical theatre company called *Senior Star Power*. Its purpose was to showcase talented people over the age of 60 and show the world that this age group is still able to be vital, productive, creative, energetic and entertaining. We are here to help others have a life filled with value, substance and meaning no matter what age they are. We believe that through artistic development, there's no limit to the level of expressive accomplishment a person can achieve.

I needed a name for these productions, so *Rockin' With the Ages* was born!

My first show was aptly called *Rockin' With the Ages I*. The first thing I needed was a theatre. I looked at 32 different venues all over LA, in search of one that could meet the specific needs of my target audience:

1. *No stairs*
2. *Wheelchair/walker accessibility*
3. *Convenient parking*
4. *Comfortable seats*
5. *Good visibility and sound*
6. *Good backstage area for talent*
7. *And of course, plenty of rest rooms*

I finally found what I was looking for at the Actors Forum in North Hollywood – a 50-seat, precious gem of a little theatre owned by a lovely former actress. She was also "of an age" and had been in show business for a long time. She believed wholeheartedly in what I was doing for our mature talent. And she realized that there was a huge audience ready and willing to make our concept of a Senior Theatrical Showcase a success.

On March 18, 2009, *Rockin' With the Ages I*, a 99 seat Equity Waiver production, had its first preview. We had a seven-week run with performances on Friday and Saturday evenings and matinees on Saturday and Sunday. I had a fabulous cast of 30 performers including Hank Garrett, a talented and famous actor/comedian as my Emcee. It was basically a variety show. It was a complete success; everyday and every night, we filled the seats.

We had it all. Talk about a mixed revue show... Everything from singers including the lovely Sue Smart and Phyllis Lovit; an exotic ribbon dancer from China, Jane Wagner; David Lara, a gentleman who had never sung before an audience (who was fabulous), a group of talented and beautiful tap dancers, the Razzmatappers; Hank Garrett, who had them rolling in the aisles; and Bobbi Stamm, a fantastic dancer doing the splits! (who's still doing it in my shows to this day.)

And most important: Everyone in the show was 60 years young and over... which set the age precedent for each of my shows from that day forward.

Wow! What a great run we had! It was fun and also a terrific learning experience for me as a producer. I learned two valuable lessons. The most important was that there's an audience out there waiting for this over-60 age group type of production. I also learned that my cast would soon become my second family, and I grew to love every one of them! We were a success! We even had to set up extra chairs for some of the shows (Shhh... don't tell the Fire Marshall!).

My next two *Rockin' With the Ages* II and III shows were also performed in 99-seat houses, still under an Equity Waiver contract. By the third show, I had learned, with many a laugh and tear, that there was a lot more to producing than I had ever imagined.

Auditioning and choosing a cast is not as easy as one might think. Putting together a group of talented performers over the age of 60 is hard to do. Thank goodness I found cast members who were dedicated and passionate about sharing my dream of showing the world that they had never lost what it takes to successfully entertain an audience.

Assembling the right production team, including a director, choreographer, writer, musical director, costume designer, lighting, sound and set designers, proved to be quite daunting. But I soon learned to ask those in other theaters, more experienced than I, who they used for their productions. Thus, I was able to put together a group of professionals who helped make my shows the successes they have always been.

My second and third shows had eight-week runs with six performances per week. These shows had the performers interacting as an ensemble, unlike the first production, which was basically a professional talent show featuring individual acts.

By the time I started work on my next show, Senior Star Power had formally become a 501(c)(3) not-for-profit corporation. We decided to call that production *The Beat Goes On* and had moved on to a lovely venue in the heart of Hollywood called the Las Palmas Theater., again in a 99 seat theatre.

There was a double cast with 15 people performing in each show. Once again, we had an eight week run with six shows per week. It was a great success. We even had a Salute to America segment at the end of each show with everyone in the audience waving an American Flag to the tune of *Yankee Doodle Dandy.*

The audience loved the energy and enjoyed the over-60 talent performing to rock, funk and rap music along with the old standards. We took Hollywood by storm! It was a smash hit, and I knew then that my dream of finding a theatre in Hollywood to house year-round senior shows would become a reality in the near future.

Due to our great success, it was now time to move to a larger venue for our next show called, We Have A Dream. This time, I rented the 326 seat Barnsdall Gallery Theatre in Hollywood. Talk about learning! Talk about growing! Talk about laughing and crying at the same time! It was all of the above!

This show too was a success; it brought Senior Star Power Productions to the attention of many of Hollywood's celebrities, elected officials and dignitaries.

After producing 15 successful musicals, I'm looking forward to producing many more musicals in our Senior Star Power Theatrical Arts Complex. It will be a 300-seat or larger venue. I am so excited! I already have an idea for the show. It will be the biggest, glitziest and most glamorous musical revue I've done to date.

Without question, growing older has taken me on the ride of a lifetime and continues to give me the best reason to live the life I've always wanted. Looking at the talented stars who are in my shows, people ask me, "What's their secret to looking so good and staying so young?" My answer is always the same: "They have coupled their talent and experience with a positive attitude, no matter what their age, thus enabling them to continue to *Get Up, Get Out, & Get a Life!*

All of my senior musical shows have always had intergenerational audience appeal. After one of the performances of *The Beat Goes On*, my videographer was asking the audience, as they were leaving, what they thought of the show. One young man about 13, who had come with his grandmother, exclaimed, "It was better than *Spiderman*. I didn't know people could dance and sing like that when they're that old. And, I didn't know they were still alive at that age." That remark made our day! We definitely feel that we give people who are in their 30's, 40's, and 50's a new perspective on what the aging process really is and can be. It's certainly something to look forward to – not to be afraid of.

By being diversified and creative in casting my shows, I give everyone a platform on which to continue to hone their skills and share their talents. Though most of my cast members are professionals, many of them, because of age discrimination, have not performed in quite a while. I am proud to say that my shows have given these people a new lease on life, and put them back, once again in the spotlight – where they belong.

Yes, my friends, I have "come a long way!" I give credit for this to the Universe for helping me reinvent myself in order to help others *Get Up, Get Out, & Get a Life!*

I remember what a friend of mine, who is 89, said: *"Life should not be a journey to the grave with the thought of arriving in a great and wonderful body, but to skid in sideways, Champagne in one hand, chocolate-covered strawberry in the other, completely used up, worn out, laughing, and yelling loud and clear, Whoa! What a ride!"*

"Pink Lady" Jackie Goldberg

Walter and me
The Dynamic Duo of Marketing

The Pink Lady:
A sales force to be reckoned with

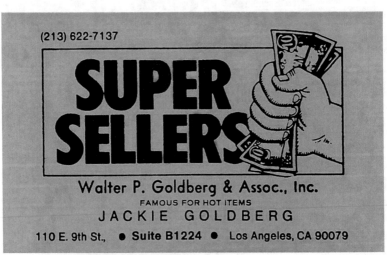

Our first business card (pink, of course)

Walter and me on a cruise to the Greek Islands

At a California Mart dinner dance

On a cruise to Mexico

209

My first grandchild Miko's Bat Mitzvah, with the whole family

Doing fine on my own

How does one get into this bed?
With good intentions and lots of money...

Condoms: Variety is the spice of life

Pink Lady makes the front page

Pink Lady wins the Ms. Senior LA County Pageant

A "Pink" Star is born

Brochure for my Seminar Series

My "Pink Boa" Attitude says it all

Those who attend my "Get Up..." Seminars are well taken care of

Welcome to the home of the "Pink Lady"

The enchanted garden of a "Pink Princess"

217

Did you expect any other license plate?

"It's all about Pink"

219

OMG!

Hot (great grand) Mama

STORY BY CHAUNA BRYANT ■ CORRESPONDENT | STAFF PHOTOS BY TINA BURCH

the contest

Ms. Senior America
pageant
Nov. 12
Imperial Palace
Las Vegas
$20 in advance
$25 at the door
www.senioramerica.org

"WE ARE STILL HERE AND WE ARE GOING TO BE PRODUCTIVE," SAYS JACKIE GOLDBERG OF SENIORS.

She calls herself the "Pink Lady", and can you, too. Jackie Goldberg wears pink ?, pink shoes, pink nail polish, pink lipstick, talks on a pink phone and lives in a pink house in Woodland Hills. Goldberg has an infectious, energetic aura that makes it possible for her to blend into crowd.

That's probably why Goldberg was named Ms. Senior East Los Angeles County ? pageant held last month at Pasadena Senior Center before an audience of 350. (The next Los Angeles pageant will held in Long Beach on Aug.

Goldberg and 12 other contestants were rated on talent, an interview with the judges and philosophy on life.

contest in Las Vegas in November.

Goldberg admitted that she was not familiar with the pageant and had to be convinced by a friend to participate. She finally did because wanted to

Las Vegas, which she visits about 10 times a year.

No, she doesn't gamble when she goes there.

"I would rather just give money to my kids and grand kids, than to hand it over to a

dressed in pink at the time.

"My husband pulled me aside and said, 'Do you want to be known in this business? Well then from now on you are going to be known as the pink lady,'" she said.

Malibu Orchid clubs. In t future, she plans to volun Kaiser Medical Center in Woodland Hills. Goldber also recently finished a c hypnotherapy under the t of Shelly Stockwell. She

Having the time of my life

221

Performing in "Grapes & Raisins" at the Stagedoor Playhouse

Me with Loni Anderson and Kate Linder

Me with Debbie Reynolds

Me with Margaret O'Brien

224

Me with Joan Rivers

Me with Ruta Lee

225

The cast of Rockin' with the Ages

226

The cast of Rockin' with the Ages II

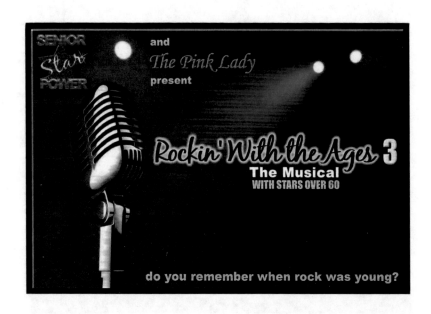

The cast of Rockin' with the Ages III

The cast of The Beat Goes On

The cast of We Have a Dream

*It's all about **Attitude***

Epilogue
IT AIN'T OVER TIL I SAY IT'S OVER

Remember, today is a new day and the first day of the rest of your life.

At this enlightened stage of my life, with five wonderful children, six super grandchildren, and four delightful great-grandchildren, I've learned how to reinvent my life to be able to live it to the fullest, with a positive attitude and a lot of gratitude. I definitely have learned that "life is for the living," so it's important to live it with energy, enthusiasm, and excitement. As Valena Broussard Dismukes says, "If women ruled the world, everything would be pink and bedazzled."

We can never go back to *before*. But who really wants to? We should all want to get to the best years of our lives, NOW - TODAY! Let's all make our future years count. WE CAN DO IT. The words "slowing down" have never been in my vocabulary. In just these

231

few past years, I started some new projects that have taken off with much success.

It all started with writing this book. Changing the perception of a group of people in this country and around the world was my main goal. The group: the over 60 community. How does one do that? In several ways. The book came first.

Next, was actually showing that those over 60 can still be sexy, scintillating, and significant. They say that a picture is worth a thousand words. And so our senior men's and lady's calendars were created. They feature everyday people "of an age" from 60 to 90; yes, I said 90! This definitely will show people that "age is only a number."

SENIOR
STAR
POWER

presents

Ladies
over 60 years young

2017 calendar

SENIOR STAR POWER

presents

Gentlemen
over 60 years young

2017 calendar

What do you do after creating calendars and writing a book? Making Senior Star Power Productions bigger and more important than ever. How? By combining the two most underserved groups in the country (seniors and veterans) and making them my number one priority.

To do that, I created a musical variety show known as "America Salutes Our Veterans." I decided to mount this production in a 1300 seat historic theater. Talk about growing from 50 seats to 1300 – now that's a challenge. This project is so much more involved than I ever imagined. BUT we did it. When good people "of an age" get together, anything is possible.

Senior Star Power Presents

I WANT YOU
TO AUDITION FOR
"AMERICA SALUTES OUR VETERANS"

A TALENT COMPETITION
Seeking SINGERS, DANCERS, COMEDIANS, MUSICIANS
MUST BE 60 YEARS YOUNG AND OVER!
CASH PRIZES!!!
AUDITIONS: AUGUST 7 & 8
Call: 818-400-2701 or Email: pinklady7@earthlink.net
Produced by Pink Lady, Jackie Goldberg and Amanda Secola

America Salutes Our Veterans with Pink Lady and Michael Moore

235

As you all know by reading this book, my main dream is to establish our very own Senior Star Power Theatrical Arts Complex. Rome wasn't built in a day (it's taken many years to become an overnight success!) So, I know that in the very near future, our theatre will become a reality.

I would love a 36-hour day and a 9 day week; that's not possible; but knowing me, I'll find a way to fit everything into the time I'm given to make my dream come true.

I'd like to tell you about a few awards I was privileged and honored to get in the past few years.

1) One was from the Southern California Motion Picture Council; with me that evening was the legendary Carol Channing receiving her award.

2) I received an award from Kathy Bee's *Touching Lives* television show. In my acceptance speech, I said that I loved proving every day of my life that age is only a number, as well as sharing my "Pink Attitude" with everyone I meet.

Receiving the Touching Lives Award

3) I was presented with the prestigious Heroes of Hollywood Award along with Judge Judy and other notables. I must tell you that receiving this honor from the Hollywood Chamber of Commerce made me feel that my work with *Senior Star Power* was now recognized by the Hollywood community. I never, ever

Two Heroes of Hollywood award winners: Pink Lady and Judge Judy

doubted that our diverse group of talented entertainers, who are committed, passionate and dedicated, could change the world's perception of how aging can be seen in a positive light.

As I said to the audience that afternoon, one of the greatest gifts you can give yourself is inspiration to make a difference in the world. It's about contribution and service. I feel that a life worth living should be devoted to something that inspires you, energizes you, and gives your life more meaning and purpose.

4)   Another award of which I am proud is the Susan B. Anthony Award, proving women do not take *No* for an answer in anything they want to accomplish.

5) When I got the Senior Care Hero Award for being the Senior Hero of the year, I felt that my dedication and commitment to the senior community was validated.

6) On another truly high note, I was honored to be the Keynote Speaker at the 23rd Annual Veterans Holiday Celebration that feeds and entertains 4,500 veterans and be able to thank our veterans and seniors for their service to our great country.

7) My latest award comes from the International Platform for Peace Organization recognizing me for "Excellence in Entertainment/Community Service." Wow! Just think, I'm only 84. I cannot wait to see what awards will come my way in the next 20 years.

I want everyone to understand that no matter what your age is, when you think young, you are young. After all these years, let's make ourselves the number one priority in our lives. It's now our turn to be happy with who we are and what we're accomplishing.

It's crazy. I feel so alive and so energetic. I know that I continue to be vital, productive and creative. I want to be able, everyday, to help others feel that same zest for life, that *joie de vivre* that I have. This lifestyle will enable us to stay active, keep healthier and living longer.

When will the world see who we really are? When will the world see that being over 60 doesn't mean the end of your life, but just a continuation on a journey? We can still bring fantastic experiences to the table. We are more than willing and able to share with everyone what we've learned from our past in order to make a better future for us all.

"I say it's time!" I see it in our homes, our workplaces, and in the country as a whole. The older adult is fast becoming an integral part of the community once again - one that is still capable of adding a positive point of view to the political, economical, social, and spiritual issues of our time.

I guess it's because I feel that 60 is the start, not the end. It's a time to be able to kick up our heels, live it up, and enjoy the many years we have left. When I first started this book, I thought, "It's not going to be a lot of pages. After all, how much do I have to say?" I was definitely mistaken. I DO have a LOT to say. And I'm proud to be able to share my life story and to yell out, loud and clear, "I'm here; learning, growing, and loving the life I've always wanted to live!"

My motto has become "age is only a number."

YES, I KNOW. I've said it many, many times, but I feel that I cannot say it enough! I hope that every one of you reading my story will adopt this philosophy. With the right attitude and gratitude, you can live your best life right now!

As I said in my Ms. Senior L.A. County parody, "To age or not to age, that is the question." It's a fantastic, positive, and passionate feeling of understanding who we are. The answer to that question can only come from within you. I hope and pray that when you find the answer, it will make your golden years as wonderful and joyous as mine are.

Here are ten resolutions that I make every year:

1. To keep my independence as long as I can.
2. To keep all my relationships on an even keel, and to keep having them!
3. To help my family whenever possible, and keep them close.
4. To try and pace myself a little better in my daily life, so I can accomplish more.
5. To watch for any "old age" signs and curb them.
6. To try to have a more nutritional and balanced eating lifestyle. To walk and exercise much more.
7. To count my blessings and love my children, cherish my friends and hold dear the "loves" in my life.

8. To take my dream of showing people that "age is only a number" all over the world.
9. To always remember to say "thank you" to the Powers That Be for giving me another day to live my life to the fullest!
10. And to acknowledge and truly thank with all my heart and soul the following people who have made me eternally grateful to be alive…

My mother and father, Fran and Scotty Rigmont, who believed I was a princess who could do it all, and so I did!

Fran and Scotty, 62 years of happiness

My dear late husband, Walter Goldberg, not only a partner, but a friend and a marketing genius, who helped me become a business success and who showed me that I could be the person I've always wanted to be.. . . . The Pink Lady.

Me and my Walter

My late partner, Arnold Arch, my soul mate, a man who helped me realize that there still is a lot of livin' to do, even in your 60's, 70's, 80's and beyond.

Me and Arnold

And my dear children and their significant others, my grandchildren, and great- grandchildren, who, each in their own way, have taught me so much about family and love, and what truly matters. I have been fortunate to have their support in all my endeavors, which has enabled me to become my own person.

My son Michael Penn, his wife Harumi, my grandson Andrew, his wife Darci, my great granddaughter Olivia, my granddaughter Miko, her partner Jill and my great granddaughter Mia

My daughter Debbie Penn, my grandson Aaron, his partner Emily, and great grandsons Malachi and Landon

*My daughter Michele Hirsch, my grandson Daniel, my grandson
Matthew and his wife Mary, and Michele's husband Howard*

My son Rick Penn, his wife Tina, and my granddaughter Nicole and her husband Matt

Let us continue on our journey through life with strength, laughter and courage. We must learn to love and be loved, and to share our time with those who matter the most. A motto that I have always followed is to "live, love and laugh my way through life." Someone once said, "Life is a succession of many moments, and to live each is to be successful." For the true spirit of life is not to try to control it, but to use what happens to better it.

The Pink Lady with Farrah MacKenzie
Inspiring a whole new generation!

My beginning years were wonderful. My middle years were full of adventure. And now, the best years are yet to come, to be able to continue to have that energy and zest for life that I had when I was 4 years old and hope to Heaven to have at 104! Then maybe, just maybe, I'll think about slowing down a bit, BUT not altogether!

I wish you the best on your journey. I know that when you realize who you truly are, you'll be able to live your life the way you want, having the time of your life. The bottom line is that I'm not buying into "It's over!" Because it ain't over til I say it's over! But most important:

*IT AIN'T OVER TIL **YOU** SAY IT'S OVER!*

I want to thank you for reading this book. I hope I've helped you understand that EVERYONE, if they want, can *Get Up, Get Out, & Get a Life!*

WE WERE NOT BORN YESTERDAY... Thank goodness!

It's not the years in your life that counts. It's the life in your years!
~ Abraham Lincoln

ACKNOWLEDGEMENT

To my late husband, Walter, whose marketing genius
created my lifelong persona as "The Pink Lady,"
and to my children, grandchildren, and great
grandchildren, I thank you for being the joy and pride in
my life.

To my friends, in and out of the entertainment world,
thank you for sharing your loyalty, support, advice and
expertise, and most important, your love, for our many
successful projects. Together, we show the world what
those over 60 can accomplish.

And, to my dear friend, Albert Sweet, along with his
business partner Craig Darian, thank you for
encouraging and helping me bring this book to "life" so
that I can share my favorite expression with all of you...

"It Ain't Over Til I Say It's Over."

Pink Lady inspires those over 60 (and all others) to continue to be vital, productive, creative, energetic, and most important, entertaining...

Pink Lady inspires and empowers our generation as well as those that will come. (LL, 73)

Pink Lady's example of living life to the fullest and her creativity has been an inspiration to me, and will continue to be so. She is a life force. (HS, 66)

Pink Lady, you're very instrumental in why we're performing again, and for that I'll never forget you. (JG, 69)

Pink, you changed my life in so many wonderful ways... brought back my confidence as a performer. You'll always be my role model to stay young and never stop believing in myself. (KS, 76)

Before Senior Star Power, I thought I was too old. Now, my life has changed. I got an agent for the first time in 40 years! (SE, 69)

Thanks to you, at age 74, I started my "career." Your whole life is about making it better for others. I am one of the many examples of this. There aren't enough "thank you's" to convey my gratitude. (RM, 76)

After a 30 year retirement, you "brought me back" on stage. I had no idea how wonderfully innovative you could make me be. I cannot express how thankful and blessed I am to be part of your vision for seniors. Yes we can! What you created is a Godsend for so many talented senior performers. Your vision has no limitations. (PL, 74)

Your positive energy is a beacon of light for all to behold. Your fortitude, drive, motivation, zest for life, beauty and charm are all bundled up into one very small package. But oh my, it is OUT OF THE BOX! (CP, 73)